CREATIVE
STRATEGIES

MARIO PRICKEN

CREATIVE STRATEGIES

IDEA MANAGEMENT FOR MARKETING, ADVERTISING, MEDIA AND DESIGN

Thames & Hudson

No matter what is written here,
the opposite is also true!

For Sebastian

CONTENTS

CONTENTS

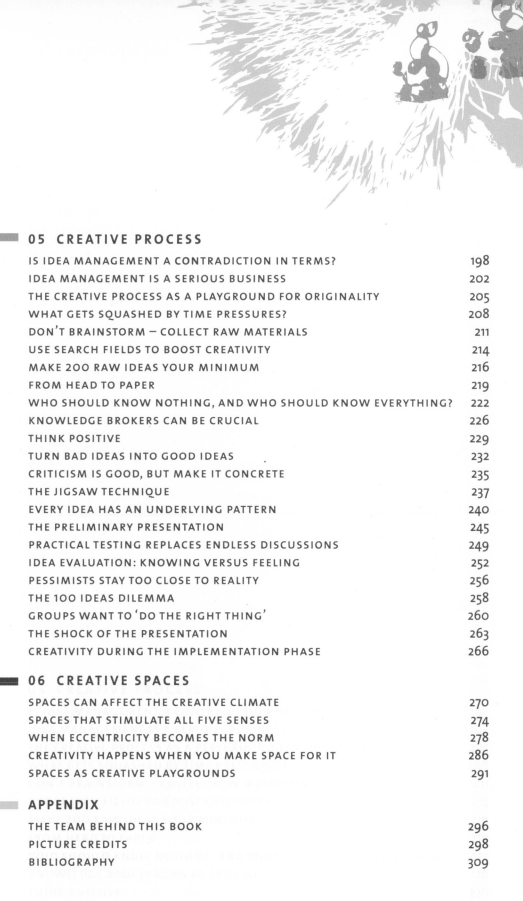

05 CREATIVE PROCESS

06 CREATIVE SPACES

APPENDIX

FOREWORD

Mario Pricken

What are creative strategies?

Creative strategies are all the methods we utilize to make our projects and campaigns a success. Mario Pricken's book is a kind of training manual, describing and explaining all the tricks of the advertising and marketing trade, challenging you by asking difficult questions and suggesting thought-provoking talking points, and showcasing 230 examples of great work from all over the world.

Who are these strategies for?

Anyone who works in the creative industries can use them, but this book has a special focus on the relationship between clients and creatives, because it's only when these two work well together that truly stunning results are possible. These strategies will help creative directors and art directors, marketing managers and anyone trying to find original solutions and build a great creative department. Creative leader-

ship is not just a matter of having good ideas. Mario Pricken draws on more than fifteen years of experience as an instructor and consultant in agencies, design studios and other firms, to present a wide variety of tools for effective idea management. At the same time he offers many fascinating insights into the alchemy of the creative process.

If you don't ask questions...

'I skate to where the puck is going to be, not to where it's been.' Ice hockey legend Wayne Gretzky's sporting rule illustrates the approach that Mario Pricken takes to creativity. Following other people rarely leads to success, let alone to original ideas.

If your job is to be constantly creative, you should devote some thought to your own creativity. How can your department be turned into an idea factory? What motivates teams to go the extra mile? How can you manage ideas instead of relying on luck and intuition? What gives a team the star status that attracts more talent and more clients?

This book asks the sort of questions that will make you rethink your assumptions about creativity, and will help you to develop a style of your own. It deliberately offers more questions than answers, because there are already plenty of books on the market that claim to give you no-fail commandments to follow.

Ideas to inspire

A boy asks his father whether fathers always know more than their sons. The father says they do. 'Daddy, who invented the Nintendo Game Boy?' asks the son. 'It was Gumpei Yokoi, I think,' replies the father. The boy ponders and asks, 'So then why wasn't it Gumpei Yokoi's dad?'

Mario Pricken sees the campaigns illustrated in this book as a challenge. They set a level against which your own creativity can be judged. If you can join their ranks, you will have contributed towards the evolution of your field. But why not turn it into a full-scale revolution? The works you see here should make you think and help you to understand how successful idea management is structured, and they should also fascinate and entertain you at the same time. But if you're thinking of copying them rather than coming up with your own ideas, perhaps you should consider changing your job!

For clients and for agencies

To date, there is scarcely any aspect of the creative process that has been given less attention than the relationship between client and creative – this very sensitive symbiotic partnership that is all-important to the quality and success of the project. This book has the shared interests of both of these groups at its very heart. If your ideas appear dull to your target group, customers, audience, visitors, members, or whoever else they are aimed at, you will fail. But take heart, the solution is right under your fingertips. All you need are the right creative strategies.

Karin and Bertram Schmidt-Friderichs

CREATIVE CULTURE

01

One of the trickiest of all relationships is that between a client and a creative: they can't get on without each other, and very often they can't get on with each other!

Surprisingly, there are plenty of people who still believe in the myth that inspiration is the province of lone geniuses working in the isolation of an ivory tower. Most agencies and design studios are organized along similar lines to this, regarding creativity as something they alone are responsible for. However, a slight change of perspective can open up the way to a completely new creative culture which offers far more possibilities than reducing the client's contribution to a simple brief and a thumbs-up sign when the job is done. Just shift the birthplace of creativity from the genius's ivory tower to the space that lies between the client and the agency. Does that seem impossible? If so, why? Just because people still feel it's a no-go area, full of pitfalls, fears and misunderstandings? It may be true this is the place where creativity can suffer most, but that's only because creatives like to close the door on the client while they're doing their own thing, and want to take almost exclusive responsibility when it comes to quality control. The fact is that the greatest potential for future success lies mainly in using and engaging the client's own resources in such a way that both sides build a creative forum in which they can help each other to generate new ideas.

▶ The Sistine Chapel: In 1508, Michelangelo Buonarroti was commissioned by Pope Julius II to paint scenes from the book of Genesis to cover the entire ceiling of the chapel. An agreement between the patron and the artist laid out the requirements of the former, the fee to be paid to the latter, and details of how the project was to proceed. If you take a close look at this contract, you will see that it dealt with very similar problems to those that confront the modern creative industries. After all those centuries, we are still wrestling with ways of ensuring the best possible cooperation between client and creative.

◀ Strategy: On the Axe Hair Crisis Relief website a presenter shows pictures of young men to a group of women. They vote on whether they approve or disapprove of each man's hair by moving to the right (for yes) or the left (for no). If the disapproval rate is hair-raisingly high, the presenter recommends an Axe product to fix the problem.

Talking point: Whenever you see a really great idea, you can be sure that its quality is the result of agreement between two partners: the client and the creative. If something strikes you as poor or merely average, the question arises: how could the weaker side of that partnership be strengthened in a way that would improve the quality of the ideas?

◀ **Strategy:** This direct mail sticks to anything it touches, and reads: 'Know the difference between being close and being inseparable'. It aims to show potential customers how the Rapp Collins agency's campaigns create a binding link between a product and a target group.

Talking point: How can the space between client and creative be changed from one of restrictive tension to one where inspiration is free to grow and can generate ideas like this one?

▶ **Strategy:** This bottle design for Taisun Water lets customers feel the natural quality of the water on all sensory levels.

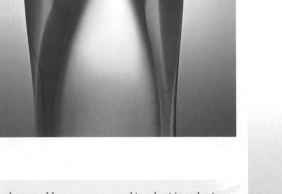

Talking point: What new approaches would your agency need to adopt in order to ensure that your future clients get involved in a manner which will increase rather than restrict the scope of their creativity?

NO MORE 'MORE OF THE SAME'

If you think and work in the same way as you've always done, chances are that you'll get the same results you've always got. If you want something completely new and need to escape from that rut, then try something different.

During the last month or so, it's pretty certain that several dozen new agencies and studios will have opened their doors. These agencies will contain the same hip creatives with the same hip job titles in the same hip premises and working in the same not-so-hip conditions as practically every other agency you know. Welcome to the realm of 'more of the same'. And more of the same on one end will almost inevitably lead to more of the same on the other. After all, how can unusual, individual ideas emerge when people keep coming together in exactly the same conference rooms, sharing exactly the same cultural background, training, professional experience, aims and ambitions? How can we expect anything different to grow out of all this sameness? What we see day after day is repetition of the same ideas, logos, events, packaging, graphics and campaigns that are barely distinguishable from one another except through their branding. As the saying goes, 'If you strike out on your own path, no one can overtake you.' Some blaze a trail. Others chase after them in the vain hope of catching up, even though the best they can hope for is to follow a well-trodden road.

Truly successful agency creatives stand out from the rest by developing a lively and inspiring creative culture which goes far beyond a few stylish pieces of artwork, flexible working hours and designer office chairs. Aim to do something different, and ask yourself the following questions, to see what you and your agency can do to turn yourselves into pioneers with an endlessly inspiring idea factory of your own.

▶ How can the way that teams cooperate be changed to make members spark ideas off one another?
▶ How can creatives get involved in projects that will motivate them to reach new heights?
▶ How can the working relationship between account handlers and creatives be redefined?
▶ What new ways can be devised to involve the client in the creative process?
▶ How can the whole atmosphere of the agency be changed so that it will become a constant source of energy and inspiration for the creative process?

If these questions don't go far enough to further your quest for a new creative culture, then try this: make a list of all the unwritten laws that underlie your chosen field. It won't be easy, because you won't be aware of most of them. Take each of these rules, and start playing with them, breaking them, or replacing them with new ones. Remember that they are nothing but ideas, and old ones at that; don't forget that they can always be jettisoned in favour of something better.

◄ **Strategy:** The Dell Summer Rocks tour held promotional events at various music festivals, in cooperation with the organizers. One of these was the 'Towel Drop': early in the morning, towels were laid out across Hermosa Beach in Los Angeles. When tourists arrived at the beach later, they took the towels away with them.

Client **Dell** | Agency Mother Experience

Talking point: What makes your own agency distinct from your competitors, and in what ways is it unusual in its field? Could a totally different approach lead to more innovative ideas?

▼ **Strategy:** This elegant winebox won several design awards. Even after opening, it keeps the wine fresh for more than two months.

Weißwein **Nr. 03**
Chardonnay
Frankreich 2005
„Vieilles Vignes"
Bourgogne

12,5 % vol. 3 Liter

Chardonnay 2005 „Vieilles Vignes" Bourgogne

3 Liter
12,5 % vol.

Talking point: What new approaches could you take with recurring topics or long-term clients in order to achieve completely different results? What aspects of in-house and out-of-house routines could you change in order to open up paths to new ideas: teams, premises, practices, contact with clients, sources of ideas, conference rooms?

How do you expect creatives to find an original way to launch a new beer, when 10,000 creatives have already spent some 600,000 hours racking their brains to do just that?

In my own view, the days of unstructured creative processes and intuitive inspiration in many branches of the industry are dead and gone. Talent is a great thing, and is a basic building block for success, but people who don't realize just how they arrived at their own creative processes tend to be stuck in a mire of clichés. For example, let's look at beer advertising. In Germany alone there are around 1,200 breweries producing around 5,000 different brands of beer. Some 3,000 of these brands are advertised. Although the first beer ads go back well over a century, to keep matters simple we'll focus on the earliest campaigns that are comparable with those of our own time.

We'll begin in 1950. Let's assume, for the sake of this little numbers game, that in 1950 about 400 brands were advertised, and this number has continuously risen to reach the present-day 3,000. And still keeping things simple, let's assume that for each brand there were two campaigns a year, for which two creatives held brainstorming sessions of two hours

each. This would mean on average that in Germany alone, around 10,000 creatives have spent around 600,000 hours dreaming up ideas for launching their beer on to the market. Now try to imagine your own team being asked to conjure up a campaign, but only being given a couple of hours in which to come up with a new idea for it. Sounds pretty ridiculous!

Nonethless, it might just work if there wasn't a huge catch: most agency creatives tend to come from the same cultural background, and so it almost goes without saying that their chains of association will be very similar to those of their predecessors. Creatives in all fields are only too aware of this phenomenon. Nowadays you need a massive dose of optimism to believe you can solve a problem like this by shutting three bright sparks in a room for a few hours and waiting for them to shout 'Eureka!' As a counter to this argument, people like to quote examples meant to prove that there are still a few exceptions that take beer advertising in completely new and unexpected directions. True enough, but what about the other 2,900 brands? And the situation becomes all the more impressive – or depressing – if we extend the market to the rest of the world. Once again, I would argue that a new creative culture means jettisoning the old romantic ideals and mystic explanations, and replacing them with strategic idea management. A precedent has already been set in fields like product development, graphic design, events planning, fashion, media, TV and film. People who keep trying to conjure up hit ideas through talent and guesswork alone will end up with nothing but the same old stereotypes.

Client Lion Nathan | Agency Publicis Mojo

▲ **Strategy:** A letter from a New Zealander living in London inspired Speight's marketing gurus to respond to his yearning for his native brew with more than just a free crate of beer. Instead, they bought a ship, signed up a crew, and transported a whole pub from New Zealand to London via New York. The 16-week trip was recorded on a website, and ended with a huge party in London.

Talking point: When teams instinctively keep opting for the same ideas, the creative culture needs to be changed and improved. What could be done to shake things up and enable a completely different approach?

'The guy who invented the first wheel was an idiot,' said Sid Caesar. 'The guy who invented the other three, HE was a genius.' But I'd say he was no cleverer than the guy who invented brakes, or the guy who worked out how to store energy in the battery.

'If I have seen a little further, it is by standing on the shoulders of giants,' wrote Sir Isaac Newton. If you are a designer, production manager or event planner and reckon that you've thought up a totally original idea, then you can't see your place in the grand scheme of things. Imagine being commissioned to design a new bottle for a soft drink. How long do you think is the human chain that leads to you and your ideas? Who was the first to dream up a container? Who discovered all the materials that you're going to use, and who invented the machines to process those materials? Who wrote the software you'll use to draw your designs? And who devised the mechanism you'll need in order to close your bottle?

No doubt you can think of a hundred similar questions. And yet creatives somehow still cling to the myth of the lone genius who strives to work out the solutions that are going to change the world. Those of us who work in the creative industries need to start playing fair with the ideas of others – think innovation rather than imitation. Look around you and it will be obvious that everything you see was once somebody's new idea, which others have proceeded to build on. Even a lone genius is only one in a long line of innovators – a member of a team without even knowing it. So try to resist the temptation to blow your own trumpet. A little humility might lead to less 'me' and more 'we'.

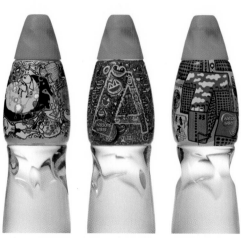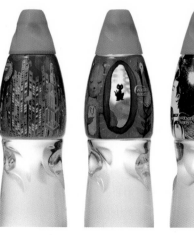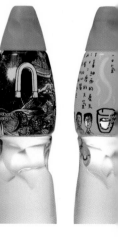

► Strategy: Twelve artists were invited to design labels for Watsons bottled water. The unusually large cap is meant to merge with the shape of the bottle.

Client **Watsons Water** | Agency **Kan & Lau Design Consultants**

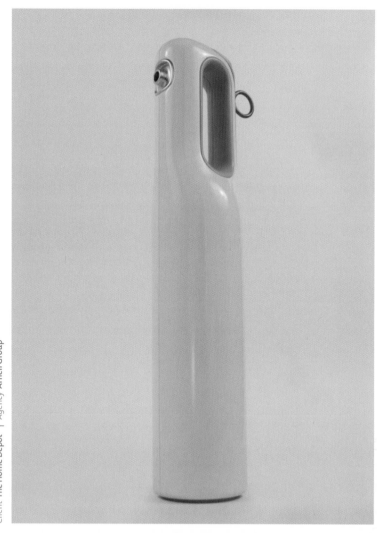

Client **The Home Depot®** | Agency **Arnell Group**

Strategy: The HomeHero revolutionized the household fire extinguisher by transforming it into an aesthetically pleasing and user-friendly appliance.

Talking point: For the most part, it is not triumphs and successes that allow us to stand on the shoulders of giants, but the countless flops, hopeless defeats and terrible mistakes that have taken place in the past. How many failures needed to occur before this product could be created?

▼ **Strategy:** The Fontegrafica printing house used this direct mail to invite their clients to Milan for a presentation of their new corporate identity. A cylinder featuring the new logo is placed in the centre of the distorted image, and reflects a group shot of the firm's staff, linking them with the new corporate design. Optical illusions such as this one have been in use for well over a hundred years.

Abbiamo il piacere di invitarLa alla presentazione della nostra nuova immagine.
24 Marzo 2005 dalle ore 18.30 • Terrazza Martini • piazza Diaz, 7 • Milano.
R.S.V.P. entro il 10 Marzo a pobox@fontegrafica.it

Client **Fontegrafica** | Agency **Cacao Design**

Your ideas can develop much more freely if you leave behind any unrealistic desire to see into the future, in the hope of avoiding mistakes that haven't happened yet or that nobody can predict or prevent.

If most of your creativity is focused on not making mistakes, you are already making a big one. This is because you're directing the energy you should be using for innovation onto something that mostly lies outside your control: the unpredictable future. The underlying motive tends to be fear of failure, and a whole industry has grown up around pandering to the insecurity and indecisiveness of those in charge by providing reassurance in the form of forecasts, customer surveys and trend analysis. What links all these together is the vain desire to see into the future and to gain control over the uncontrollable. The result is that an increasing number of firms follow current trends and standards, because swimming with the tide seems to offer the best chance of avoiding blunders. They would rather take the tried and trusted path than risk taking a new one and tripping over, and as a consequence they come up with designs and products that are only superficially different from those of their competitors. A truly creative culture inevitably means taking risks, but those involved should ask themselves how they can turn negatives into positives, so that in the long term they can gain an advantage over the competition simply by being different.

▼ **Strategy:** A specially-built TV studio for the gameshow *1 vs 100*, in which a single contestant takes on 100 opponents. Using general knowledge, tactics and strong nerves, the winner can potentially amass over £200,000 in prize money.

Client Magic Media Company | Agency Procon Event Engineering GmbH

Talking point: If you want to know if your agency has the courage to be creative, ask your colleagues the following question as regularly as you can: What do you think would be the worst possible outcome if you came up with a new idea that failed? What would be the consequences for your own career? The underlying mood of the answers – which should be given anonymously – will reflect the unspoken fears of the team, and the current state of your agency's creative culture.

this song is a world first; a song outside the limits of human hearing, produced solely for your dog's ears. they can hear it, but you can't, so please play this cd at normal volume.

thanks to you, this song will go straight to the top of the pups.

all proceeds to the SPCA

SPCA

a very silent night

SPCA

do not play at excessive volume

▲ **Strategy:** New Zealand's Society for the Protection of Animals issued a Christmas CD with a song recorded on a very high frequency that was audible only to dogs. With an advertising budget verging on zero, the song, 'A Very Silent Night', not only got dogs dancing and wagging their tails, but also attracted a great deal of publicity and brought in a flood of donations.

Talking point: Under what circumstances would you have had the courage to follow through an idea like this? What conditions need to be established for your creatives to feel they can take risks of this kind?

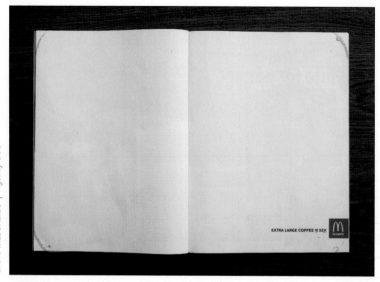

EXTRA LARGE COFFEE 16 SEK

◄ **Strategy:** With this exaggerated two-page ad, McDonald's draws attention to its Extra Large Coffee.

Talking point: Can you devise three rules that could be imposed to automatically stop your team from taking any risks?

CREATIVITY WITHOUT MISTAKES IS IMPOSSIBLE

If you ever come across an agency that has never made a terrible mistake before, you can be sure it's an agency that has never produced anything original.

Problems and failures are an unavoidable consequence of new ideas, but they can also be inspiring in themselves. Interestingly, the subject of mistakes is often taboo when it comes to discussions between clients and agencies, but without recognition of the possibility of disaster there can never be any creativity worthy of the name. A sensible first step, therefore, is for client and agency to get together before the project begins, and to reach a clear understanding as to how they will both deal with problems, with a view to turning obstacles into advantages. Clients need to explain exactly what they want, and must set the limits on the degree of originality that they are prepared to accept. What will never work is a commission like the following: 'We want you to design something that's completely new and revolutionary and yet at the same time a huge cliché that has already proved to be a surefire success.' If the agency agrees to a contradictory demand like that, it will be giving the creative team a totally impossible problem that can only be solved by some ghastly compromise. It can be a valuable exercise to discuss mistakes after they have been made. Many clients and creatives miss this opportunity by trying to hide their failures under a cloak of silence. Mistakes,

however, can provide new and worthwhile insights which may give the agency an edge over the competition. Together, client and agency should work out where, how, when and why things went wrong, and look for the positive potential in negative experiences. An open acknowledgment of mistakes will strengthen the ties between both parties in the long run.

How NOT to profit from your mistakes:

▶ Forget the fact that you can't be creative without taking risks.

▶ Don't tell anyone that they can learn from their mistakes.

▶ Make sure that mistakes are viewed only as problems and never as potential opportunities.

▶ Remember that the old ways are the best when it comes to avoiding mistakes, especially when they stifle creativity.

▶ Use other people's mistakes to show how clever and knowledgeable you are.

▶ In your quest for absolute perfection, show zero tolerance towards the slightest error.

▶ Set very tight deadlines, so that there can be no time for trial and error.

Product recall.

Volkswagen Golf Type I, 1974 model

It has been shown that, due to vibration, the **closing mechanism of the glove compartment** can be subject to wear. In the long run, in some cases, this might result in a more difficult handling of this mechanism. Even though no complaints have been registered, Volkswagen is making Golf Type I owners aware of this, as a precaution.

As this is not in line with the high standards of quality that Volkswagen has for its products, owners of the above-mentioned model are requested to go to www.volkswagen.nl/recall before 12 January 2008. If necessary, Volkswagen will have the closing mechanism **replaced free of charge**. Volkswagen regrets any inconvenience caused. This is why Volkswagen offers dissatisfied customers **free servicing** for their car as compensation.

Volkswagen emphasizes that this only applies to the Volkswagen Golf Type I, 1974 model.

Once again, Volkswagen offers its apologies for any inconvenience caused.

Pon's Automobielhandel B.V. (Volkswagen importer)

◀ **Strategy:** This ad for the Dutch car importer Pon's appeared in daily newspapers and turned an apparent mistake into a means of emphasizing Volkswagen's reliability.

Talking point: What effect would an open acknowledgment of mistakes have on relationships with clients, and on the quality of your creative team's ideas?

◀ **Strategy:** This Dove commercial uses timelapse photography to show how an ordinary-looking girl can be turned into a billboard model. The ad ends by pointing out that it's no surprise our view of beauty is distorted, and promotes Dove's approach to natural beauty.

▼ Strategy: The 'Blocked Nose' campaign illustrates the problem solved by Otrivin nasal spray.

Talking point: Clients who try to steer clear of mistakes at all costs are unlikely to have a culture of creativity. Any agency that is aware of this will either have to toe their line, or will stay true to its own standards and wave goodbye to clients of this kind.

Talking point: Who is responsible for mistakes, problems and unforeseen difficulties? In any project there should be at least two people in the hot seat: one representing the client, and one the agency. Without these two particular individuals, there can be no culture of mistakes and hence no proper culture of creativity from which original ideas can emerge.

STAYING OPEN TO ALL APPROACHES

If you're looking for new forms of packaging but surround yourself with nothing but packaging experts, you can be sure that you won't come up with anything new, just as Ralph Baer would never have come up with the first games console if he'd focused on nothing but board games.

Designers like nothing more than to surround themselves with other designers, and they don't trust anyone from outside. This insularity is common to many branches of the creative industry, and the solution is to open the doors and windows and let in some fresh air to revitalize your team. You should be prepared to invite people totally unconnected with the field of design to submit their ideas, because their very lack of experience might bring you something so original that it will revolutionize your approach. If your team have no desire to take such a step, you may find that others will leap in ahead of you. The inspiration for the next Big Idea can come from anywhere – not just from tried and trusted sources. Keep this in mind when you buy the latest specialist book, plan the next conference, sign up for the next project, or take on new staff. Anyone whose aim is to build up a truly creative culture ought to be prepared to open up the agency to new influences – even if the benefits might not be immediately apparent.

Client **LACOSTE** | Agency **Zaha Hadid Architects**

▼ **Strategy:** Lacoste introduced a new shoe collection designed in collaboration with acclaimed architect Zaha Hadid.

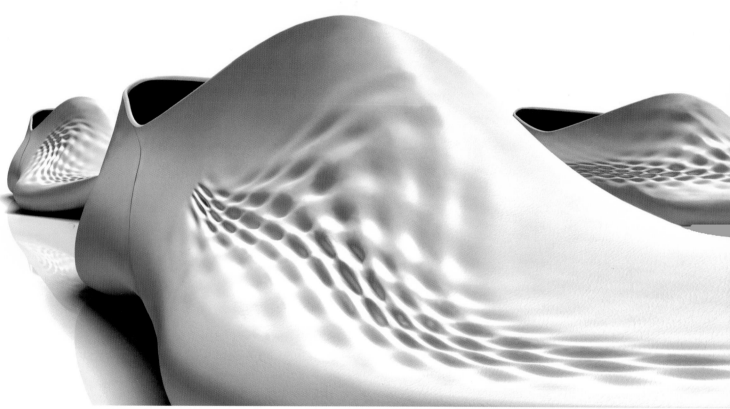

Talking point: How would the creative culture of your agency be affected if you were to invite experts from completely different fields to help you seek new ways of solving old problems?

◄ **Strategy:** It has become a tradition for Evian to work with international designers. One of the latest is Jean Paul Gaultier, who designed this striking bottle for mineral water.

Talking point: What completely new forms of collaboration would be conceivable in your field? Now take one step further. What frontiers have never yet been crossed in your quest to open up new approaches for products, teams, companies, materials or technical innovations?

▶ **Strategy:** This packaging for Osiris sneakers was designed to look like a ghetto blaster.

Talking point: Can you think of any specific people who might inject new ideas into your team? Think of someone you've never thought of before – or even someone you would previously have excluded from your team.

PRESS THE RESET BUTTON AND START AGAIN

Thinking outside the box? When asked to do so, most people simply switch from one box to another. Maybe it's a slightly larger or more colourful box, but it will still be a box that other people have used. Try leaving all the boxes behind, and go back to a place where there were no boxes at all.

Direct marketing, for instance, is one sort of box. The moment your expert hears the expression, it brings to mind a whole heap of experiences and rules relating to how a campaign should be planned and executed. Specialists are all too aware of these rules, but the most restrictive rules of all are those that people are no longer aware of. These are the unwritten rules of the business. You will find this phenomenon in every branch of marketing, advertising, media and design. That is why it would be extremely useful if direct marketing specialists, for instance, could occasionally try to forget everything they know and say: 'Direct marketing? What's that? Never heard of it!' The exercise would be even more beneficial if it was carried out together with the client. Don't act as if you already knew all there is to know. This apparent omniscience only leads to repetition of the same old routines. A truly creative culture means going against the tacitly accepted norms and taking things right back to the start, and never being afraid to ask the most naive of questions because these could produce brand new answers. Reinvent direct marketing, so that you can get rid of all the clichés. Seek out the oldest and most sacrosanct laws that govern your field, and have fun slowly taking them apart. Then start afresh, as if this were the very first time anyone had ever thought of such a thing as direct marketing, and do it in a way that's different, contemporary, even radical.

◄ **Strategy:** This landscape gardener's business card is in fact a sample packet of grass seeds, which conveys a great deal more than just contact information. How could this idea be expanded to encompass the whole concept of business cards? Be as extreme as you like.

Talking point: Leave conventional ideas behind and switch to new ways of thinking. Don't compromise. It doesn't matter how big or how small the projects are, you should always ask if an apparently new idea could be given an even more radical form that could revolutionize a product or a field.

▶ **Strategy:** How are you today? This was the question asked by the artist Erik Krikortz on his website. The answers were projected onto a high-rise complex in Stockholm in the form of a light show.

Each colour expressed a particular mood, on a scale of one to seven. Altogether, 200,000 people from different Swedish cities expressed their feelings in this colourful manner.

Talking point: Every so often you should go right back to the creative basics. Sometimes it can be useful to completely reject existing concepts of TV, packaging, newsletters or trade fairs in order to reinvent them from scratch. Have you ever considered what circumstances might allow you to stop trying to improve old ideas and start all over again?

◀ **Strategy:** Somewhere in the world, a child dies every 15 seconds due to a lack of safe drinking water. To draw attention to this tragic statistic and to attract donations, Belgian

TV interrupted several live shows at peak viewing time with a little boy suddenly running onscreen and drinking the water provided for the presenter or studio guests.

BREAK DOWN THE BARRIERS IN YOUR MIND

Anyone making a film today could also be setting a fashion, and anyone creating a fashion design could also be influencing an entire lifestyle. Stylish lifestyles are promoted by huge events, and events themselves attract advertising. People who design ad campaigns may influence packaging, and someone who develops packaging may well inspire a new product.

In the creative culture of the future, it will become essential not only to understand the wider connections between things, but also to create connections by deliberately removing the borders between fields and disciplines. Everything is linked to everything else because the whole world is now a single stage, and modern technology allows its performances to be increasingly eclectic. Unfortunately, many creatives are still stuck within the narrow confines of their own particular arena. When it comes to developing ideas, they find it impossible to leap over the fence or, even better, pull it down in order to merge different territories into one. If you want to see things on a broader scale, you should try to base initial targets and briefs on a bird's-eye view of the whole landscape. Once you have grasped the big picture, it will be far easier for you to break down barriers and establish new connections. But as well as breadth, you should strive for depth – dissect the project, look into every detail, and keep asking yourself what methods and tools could be combined in novel ways in order to reach the standards of excellence required.

Credits ProSieben Sat.1 Media AG

▼ Strategy: A TV show devised around the theme of Lego, with children and celebrities taking part in exciting or silly adventure games.

Talking point: What angles can you find to show off the qualities of a successful product, a new material, an established technology, or a particular service? In what ways have they never been used before? How can you ensure that your team will automatically incorporate this kind of lateral thinking into their creative culture?

How can there be any advantage in forcing product developers, designers, marketing researchers and managers, packaging designers and advertising experts to work like a faceless factory production line?

Before it reaches the market, a modern product goes through clearly defined phases of development. A consequence of this is a lack of consultation between companies, departments and individuals working on the same project. A packaging designer, for instance, will hardly ever be influenced by the technicians working on the product itself, and the product designer will hardly spare a thought for the marketing people. This rigid compartmentalization may have some advantages, but for the most part it actually hinders the chances of the product receiving the best possible launch. The sooner all departments come together, the greater the potential for improvements and innovations that they would not have been able to devise if they worked in isolation. This is networking at its best. If you have a new project, make it a priority to bring all sides together as early in the game as possible, and try to convince clients that it's in their own interests to take part in this kind of free and frank exchange of ideas.

Strategy: This ski design was developed by the creative consultancy KISKA, from the product itself to the ad campaign and the trade fair launch.

Strategy: As one of Europe's leading agencies, KISKA oversees the whole process from design to marketing through what it calls Integrated Design Development (IDD). This means an interdisciplinary approach at every phase, including market research, development and design, packaging and advertising.

Talking point: What methods can you devise to bring teams, departments and companies together in order to ensure maximum success at every phase of product development?

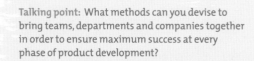

What do you regard as the principal strength of your agency? What do you sell, and why do clients come to you rather than someone else? Is it your creativity? Then take note of what separates the urgent from the important.

Agencies that are short on creativity often focus on fast or routine projects rather than on the quality of their ideas. Perhaps subconsciously, they see the creative process as something of a waste of time, and so they find all kinds of excuses for brushing it aside. Anyone who skimps on investment in the raw material we call 'ideas' may never miss a deadline, but the result will be a poor standard of inventiveness, or mere imitation of other more exciting ideas. This is where the creative department has to distinguish between what is important and what is urgent. Not all projects that seem urgent are necessarily important, and vice versa. If the daily grind has long since drained your team of all originality, ask this vital question: What position does your agency want to hold in the marketplace? Do you represent a quick turnover at any price, or brilliant ideas expertly executed? The bad news for those who think originality comes second is the fact that in future far more time and energy will need to be spent on ideas than was the case even ten years ago. For more details on this, see Chapter 5.

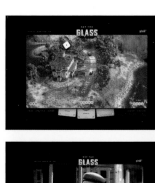

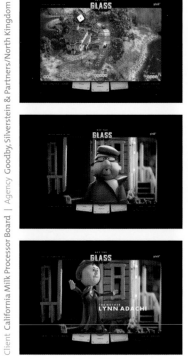

Client California Milk Processor Board | Agency Goodby, Silverstein & Partners/North Kingdom

◀ **Strategy:** The online game 'Get the Glass' makes players aware of the importance of milk for family health. The aim is to help the Adachi family to find a way into Fort Fridge in order to get a glass of milk. The winners are sent an attractive milk glass.

Talking point: Do all the people involved in the project have a clear vision of the time and energy needed for each task, whether simple or complex?

▶ **Strategy:** In this print campaign, the Nissan Qashqai seems well equipped to deal with the dangers of the urban jungle.

Client Nissan | Agency TBWA\Paris

Talking point: At what point does the simple but original concept underlying the ad actually emerge – during the ideas phase, or the implementation phase?

Client **tesa AG** | Agency Jung von Matt

tesa✓ **Pack** ultra strong®

◄ Strategy: Using ultra-strong packaging tape, an artist created images representing strength.

Talking point: What happens if a team keeps cutting back on its creative processes or cutting them short? Is there an increase in the quality and quantity of ideas, or in the originality and clarity of the raw materials?

*In the creative industries, chance
should not just be a method –
it should have a method.*

It may sound paradoxical, but rules create freedom. In most creative companies, there is still resistance against the shift from the concept of creativity as something romantic and intuitive to that of a clearly defined creative process. It is almost regarded as a betrayal of the myth if we claim to be able to manage our ideas and guide the creative process. And yet no system can more easily be thrown off balance than one that works through pure intuition, without any understanding of how to cope with time pressures, nebulous targets, brainstorming, and all the related problem areas. The high price that some agencies have to pay for this starry-eyed attitude can be seen in the fact that, all too often, unspecific goals and disorganized meetings lead to unsuitable concepts that force the team to keep going back to square one. There can be four or five false starts before anyone comes up with a solution that is acceptable to the client. The cost of all this is rarely borne by the client, and in some cases can lead to financial meltdown for the agency. Professional monitoring of ideas can cut the expense and make the path to success shorter. But quite apart from the commercial and financial aspects, I firmly believe that this sort of discipline can lead to a rise in quality and to better teamwork than the purely intuitive approach.

ALASKA: MC

► Strategy: The two
pages of this ad are stuck
together at the point
where the mother's nipple
meets the baby's mouth.
When the pages are
opened, a piece of paper
is torn from the nipple
and sticks to the baby's
mouth. A striking way of
promoting a lotion to
soothe sore skin and
prevent infection.

BREASTFEEDING HURTS

See, your baby is hungry 12 times a day, and that
much of breastfeeding makes your nipples very
sensitive. They become sore and may even crack.
But it will not be a torture, if you use "Garmastan"
lotion before and after the feeding. Made out of essential oils, the lotion softens the nipple, makes skin
smoother and prevents infection.

GARMASTAN®

Talking point: What do your colleagues fear they might lose if the creative
process is given structure and the romantic myth of creativity discarded?

◄ **Strategy:** This action-packed promo lets viewers know about a week of TV documentaries on Alaska.

Talking point: How can your team ensure consistent quality if they have to deal with a large number and variety of projects?

▶ **Strategy:** In the event of an accident, we would all instinctively protect our heads with our hands. This basic idea underlies the 'Change Your Head' campaign from helmet manufacturers BYE.

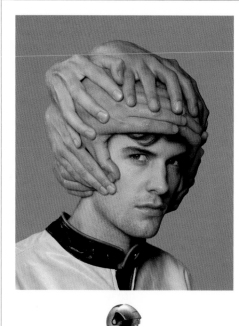

Client **BYE HELMETS** | Agency 1861UNITED

Talking point: What is the monthly price your agency pays for a disorganized creative process that forces the team to start some projects all over again?

WHAT SERVICES ARE PROVIDED BY A SERVICE PROVIDER?

Do you follow the ideas of your client, or does the client eagerly follow yours? The balance is largely determined by the self-image of the service provider.

Railway porters and heart surgeons both provide a service. To which of them would you compare your agency? Many agencies simply follow their clients' instructions and are keen to keep them happy, even if the result is a drastic drop in quality. Others sit down with their clients and advise them on what they consider to be the best option, although this may lead to major differences of opinion. In extreme cases, some creatives would rather lose a client than harm them by agreeing to a half-hearted compromise. No patient would ever dream of giving a heart surgeon advice just before an operation. But if you don't tell the porter where you want him to put your luggage, you may never see it again. So what do you understand by

service provision, and what do you consider your particular strengths? Many creatives regard themselves as their clients' porters, and meekly do as they're told. However, this may lead clients to believe that they're dealing with a weak and incompetent partner, and can make them even more inclined to assume full control. Nevertheless, someone who can demonstrate genuine flair will quickly earn the trust of clients and will be able to encourage them to go along with more unusual and even risky recommendations. What clients often find lacking in the creative industries is the ability to give sound advice and to set in motion a solid creative process that will encompass all aspects of the task that lies ahead.

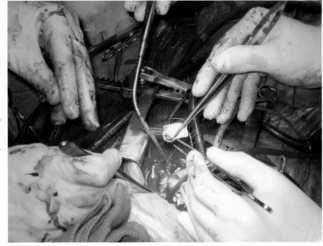

Talking point: Would you happy to undergo an operation by a heart surgeon who asked for your advice? And here's a tip for heart surgeons: you can assume that the only sort of patient who will give you advice is one who doesn't trust you to do your job.

◄ **Strategy:** The design of the Pritt MyStyle Correction Roller transforms an ordinary office tool into a designer product which is also extremely efficient and easy to use.

Client **Pritt/Henkel** | Agency **Waacs Design & Consultancy**

Talking point: Account handlers are increasingly used as client advisers. Without their input, the results of many creative projects would belong to the realm of art rather than the domain of innovative communication. What kind of creative services do you think will earn the approval of your future clients?

◀ **Strategy:** In order to demonstrate to the decision-makers from the packaging industry how BASF's innovative materials could enhance emotional appeal, individuality and convenience, the entire location for an event was transformed into a huge package.

Client **BASF SE** | Agency **circ**

Talking point: To what degree would your team be prepared to dismantle or dilute an extraordinary concept just to preempt possible objections from clients, to comply with their personal tastes or influence a power struggle within their own company? Define what your service is aiming to achieve.

Client New Zealand Transport Agency
Agency Clemenger BBDO

  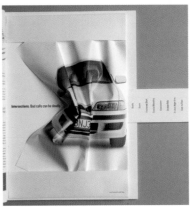

◀ **Strategy:** 'Intersections. Bad calls can be deadly.' The further you pull the tab on this road safety ad, the more serious the injuries listed on the tab become. The list reads: 'Cuts to face. Broken right arm. Broken ribs. Concussion. Cranial bleeding. Fractured skull. Death.'

Talking point: Where are the quality criteria of your creative department laid down? How do your clients and colleagues know the values that your agency represents?

ARTISTS OR TROUBLESHOOTERS?

Creative excellence is most easily displayed when creatives transform initial problems into brilliant solutions. All you need do is seize the opportunity.

First the bad news. Opportunities do not come to you – you have to see them first, and then grab them. And therein lies the true spirit of creativity. Thinking about a client's project in terms of opportunities is not a luxury but an essential process, and requires an inner conviction to lay the foundations for a successful outcome. Projects are often bedevilled by tricky side issues like inadequate information, unsuitable partners, time shortages, over-cautious colleagues, under-budgeting, inconvenient deadlines, overly narrow parameters, lack of motivation or inattention to detail. Once you start to complain, the writing is on the wall. In many branches of the creative industries, people have forgotten that work contracts entail solving problems of this kind instead of whining about them. A creative culture demands a creative climate, in which every opportunity is grasped in the quest for the right outcome. But if you can only exercise your creative talents under perfect conditions, you may as well hand in your notice and go and be an artist. On the other hand, if you see yourself as a troubleshooter and problem-solver, you can take charge instead of giving yourself a hundred excuses for not being able to fulfil your potential as a creative genius.

► **Strategy:** In 1970, the crew of Apollo 13 were forced to turn a problem into an opportunity in the most shocking way. On their way to the moon, there was an explosion on board the ship, which threatened to cut off all the oxygen, electricity and water supply in the Odyssey command module. One of the immediate tasks was to repair the overloaded air purification system. To build a suitable adaptor, however, the only materials they had were those already on board. These included things like bags, sticky tape and flight plans. Together with the control centre in Houston, the crew worked out a successful method of constructing an adaptor. On 17 April 1970, Apollo 13 landed in the Pacific, where the crew were safely picked up by the USS *Iwo Jima*.

Source NASA Center

Talking point: How can you ensure that a team will transform unexpected problems into opportunities instead of complaining about them?

Credit Dyson Design

► **Strategy:** James Dyson noticed that conventional vacuum cleaners lost their suction as the bag filled up, and so he decided to reinvent the machine. After years of experiments and 5,127 protoypes, he was at last ready to launch his invention on the market: the first bagless vacuum cleaner. Initially, his idea was resisted or rejected by other manufacturers, but in the meantime Dyson had already left many of his competitors behind.

Talking point: What is missing from a creative culture if the predominant view is that people would like to pursue creative ideas, but they are not given the opportunity? Is it due to working conditions, the attitude of team members, or a lack of cooperation between clients and the agency?

IS CREATIVITY ON DEMAND REALLY POSSIBLE?

There are times and places in which wonderful things happen simply because everything is right: the atmosphere, the task, the motivation, the team, the space, and a common goal. Some call this serendipity, but others call it a creative culture.

A creative culture becomes visible and tangible when a group of people agree on a set of values that will lead to a far wider range of opportunities than they could ever access on their own. Sometimes this combination comes together by chance, but sometimes there is a conscious effort to produce it. The fact that it is not always easy can be seen from a closer look at the cultures of some top performers in the creative arena. The animation studios Pixar and the ad agency Bartle Bogle Hegarty base their entire approaches on factors such as motivation, vision and the desire to produce

something unique. This inner conviction has become second nature to everyone who works for them. But it would be strange to think that creativity could be laid out in mission statements, brought to life by means of checklists, or imposed on a team by way of short-term additional training. Clearly, more than that is needed.

However, if you can set up a motivating playing field in which your team is free to make all kinds of unexpected moves, you will soon see the emergence of a creative culture that is capable of producing an almost endless stream of innovative ideas.

Client Langmanyishen Limited Company
Agency SKSK architects

Talking point: Just as it seems absurd to demand spontaneity, it may on the surface seem absurd to demand creativity. What long-term strategies do you have in your agency to ensure that creativity is always an integral part of your approach?

▲ **Strategy:** These posters for the WWF (World Wide Fund for Nature) show endangered species armed with hunting weapons. Laser sights shine onto the clothes of passers-by, as if the animals in the posters are aiming at them.

Talking point: Music history records several legendary jam sessions which produced unforgettable songs and unique concerts – events when absolutely everything clicked. Magic moments like those simply can't happen on demand. They arise from a free and unforced interaction between all the participants. Can the members of your team inspire one another in the same way, and are they aware of the factors required to create a productive climate of this kind?

CHANGING THE WAY WE DO BUSINESS

The basic job of the creative industries is to come up with great ideas. So isn't it surprising how many so-called creatives are resistant to change, and loudly oppose any innovations that might lead to new ideas?

Those who demand creativity are not necessarily open to new ideas. This paradox is a common experience in agencies, design studios, fashion firms and TV companies all over the world. And yet the same rules apply to agencies as to everyone else: if you can't adapt voluntarily to a changing environment, sooner or later you will either be forced to do so, or you will go under. When I'm training teams in idea management, I often hear creatives say how great it would be to work in a different way and replace the old systems with something new and original. But in the same breath they tell me that change is unfortunately out of the question – they've always worked in the same

unstructured manner, with the same predictable results. This can often lead to frustration, lack of motivation, and ultimately people either resigning or being fired. There are three possible outcomes when this situation arises: 1) creatives must find colleagues within the firm who will support them in the drive for a new creative culture; 2) the downward spiral to failure; 3) leaving the agency and setting up a new business that fits their own vision. My advice is to try and change the rules in your own arena. Don't forget that at one time the agency you're working for now was nothing more than a vision. So why shouldn't the old vision be replaced by a new one?

◀ Strategy: In order to demonstrate the effectiveness of a new detergent, Unilever produced a direct mail with a gift. However, the gift was not the sample of the product, but the T-shirt that it was wrapped in. When the recipient used the detergent, a single wash brought the T-shirt back to its original dazzling whiteness.

Talking point: In many cases, new ideas are not killed off by your colleagues, but by the rigid structures that have become entrenched as a result of past successes. Can you pinpoint any rules and routines in your own agency that create resistance to innovation?

▶ Strategy: Easyweb is a company aiming to conquer new territory with their large-scale video projections. They use original animations and videos to blend in with all kinds of surfaces and buildings.

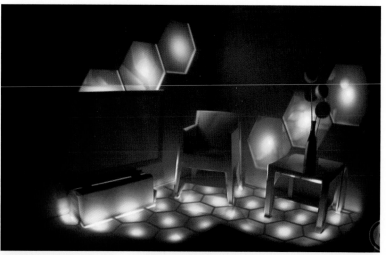

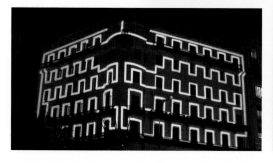

Talking point: If your existing team or agency offers no opportunity for innovation, it might be useful to propose setting up a kind of laboratory, in which new ideas can be developed without restriction and then tested for their practicality. If people don't like the idea, remind them of Charles Darwin: it's not the strongest or the cleverest who survive, but those who are best able to adapt to a changing world.

CREATIVE TEAM LEADING

02

Do you think you can simply order your team to summon up the pioneering spirit, inspiration, courage and creativity that started the agency off in the first place?

Would you like to be part of a project in which you were asked to develop new entertainment formats for the biggest stars of the music business, so that you could work with them on developing new brands and products? Or would you prefer a project whose primary aim was to increase this year's quarterly profits by 2.7 per cent over last year's? Which of these two do you think would be more likely to set pulses racing? How can innovation, inspiration, creativity and courage be the watchwords of a team whose leaders' sole concern is the quarterly balance account? The directors of any agency need to be constantly aware of the fact that creativity is not available on demand, but has to be ignited by enthusiasm and vision. An inspirational vision will fire people up, because they will see their chance to become part of something worthwhile, something that might blaze a trail for the future. If the only vision is spreadsheet columns showing profit and loss, the long-term result can only be loss. However, it is also obvious that once you start moving into new terri-

tory, you will need to balance your freedom with critical analysis – visions that totally lack down-to-earth realism will quickly dissolve into thin air.

The Instant Vision Machine: Visualize your dream now!

How can a dream come true if you don't have a dream in the first place? Or are you one of those people who already has a very detailed vision? Where exactly do you want to lead your team? What amazing prospects lie there for you all in the Promised Land? And why should anyone want to follow you there? This is your chance, right at this moment: focus your mind on what you believe, on your dreams and your values. Work your way through the following three phases, and make your vision irresistible!

1. In a few sentences, describe your vision for your agency as a whole, for an individual project, or for your own department. Refine those sentences until they

contain the absolute essence of your vision, in a way that will attract and inspire the reader. In the end, you should be left with just one sentence. But if the sheet of paper remains empty, or contains merely a list of sensible statements or existing projects, start again.

2. Use this single sentence to imagine a scene, maybe a short film, depicting your vision of a future in which your dream has come true. You should visualize it in full colour, vivid, positive, and just the way you want it to be. Now ask yourself what it is that makes your vision so powerful and magnetically attractive. What aspects of it absolutely demand to be made real? Your vision must be so convincing that you yourself can't resist the urge to make it come true.

3. Now ask yourself what effects this vision will have once it becomes reality. Who might have problems with it, or be harmed by it, or oppose it, and for what reasons? As you answer this question, you may find major obstacles that could jeopardize the fulfilment of your dream. Then you must adjust it, work out original solutions to the problems, and perhaps even start again from scratch. But do it now!

Credits Apple, Inc.

◄ **Strategy:** All Apple products are underpinned by a vision that unites technological innovation with an unmistakable concept of design.

Talking point: Visionaries seldom begin with a strategic plan for a surefire success, but they start with a dream that inspires others to do things out of the ordinary. The vision may be embodied by a person or an unusual project. Does your team ever get the chance to work on totally original projects? Visions are the fuel that powers innovation.

▲ **Strategy:** The Red Bull Air Race World Series has established itself as a new kind of sport and is now covered by some 70 TV channels. It all began through one man's vision and passion for flying: Dietrich Mateschitz, founder of Red Bull.

Talking point: In order to make a dream come true, first you have to wake up, and then you have to describe your dream to other people. The clearer the vision and its aim, the more enthusiastic your team will be, and so the more creative power you will unleash.

CREATIVITY IS THE TEAM LEADER'S PRIORITY

Creativity arises when you make a conscious decision to be creative. But if people are working on the project and have taken a completely different decision, you need to know about it.

Creativity should be a team leader's concern first and foremost because it requires an initial decision followed by the determination to follow that decision through. If the top échelons of your agency are in favour of innovation, that will give the dream its best possible chance of coming true. Leadership means showing others the way and acting as the spearhead of the mission. This applies just as much to the client as to the agency. It is naive to assume that you only need a few designers, copywriters, art buyers and photographers to make up a team that will guarantee success. Creative team leading is not just a matter of directing the creative department. The leader must convince everyone involved in the project, including the client and the chief executive, that originality is the key to success, and although this may sound obvious, a lack of this kind of integration is the most common cause of mediocre results and failure.

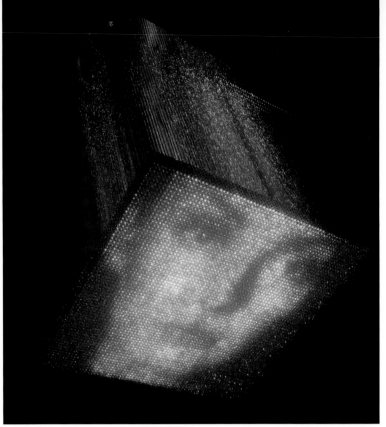

► Strategy: In the Svarovski Crystal Palace, designer Tokujin Yoshioka installed 'Stardust', a futuristic chandelier made of almost 5,000 fibre-optic sideglow tails that carry images to the tips of more than 18,000 crystals.

Talking point: A fertile climate of creativity must be initiated and constantly encouraged by those at the top. What would be a good first step for you to take in order to create a climate like this and allow it to flourish?

Client Designboom and Procter & Gamble 'Reinvent' competition | Creatives Tommaso Ceschi & Francesca Del Vigo

◄ Strategy: This 'dumbbell' packaging for Mr Clean visually expresses the brand value of strength. In keeping with this concept, it also has another use: the empty container can be filled with sand or water and used as part of a personal fitness programme.

Talking point: Have you ever thought of asking your team what they think could be done to ensure that original ideas became integral to the leadership culture? Both client and agency can benefit from knowing what is needed.

▶ **Strategy:** This print ad shows how Amway 'Shine Like New' car polish makes an old Beetle shine like a brand-new model.

Client **Amway Thailand** | Agency **Young & Rubicam**

Client **MINI** | Creative **Cees Smit**

◀ **Strategy:** The roof of this Mini exhibition stand is hung with dozens of fabric tubes, each of which holds three inflatable balls. They take up most of the stand and create an unusual sense of space.

THE COURAGE TO LEAD

The worst kind of routine is when the creative director always knows in advance exactly what the client wants to see.

In many agencies, people no longer ask which option is the best, but simply which one the client is most likely to accept. This stick-in-the-mud timidity is often glossed over as 'experience' or 'good customer relations'. As a creative team leader, you should have the courage to resist the easy way out, because by rejecting familiar pathways, you may open up far more productive avenues. Let yourself be surprised – at least that will be more exciting than letting yourself be bored! But of course taking risks doesn't mean rushing into something utterly stupid. You must be prepared to take the consequences of your decisions. By doing so, you will send out all the right signals to your team – that you have a mind of your own, and that you will also encourage them to think for themselves. If your decisions then lead to success more often than not, you will take on star charisma and people will want to follow your lead. On the other hand, it can be the loneliest job in the world, so are you prepared to take the heat when it comes, and even to lose your role? In some countries (and companies), it is a major part of the cultural tradition to discuss all projects on a democratic basis. Creative directors are often keen to abide by this convention, because it means that everyone shares responsibility. The consequence, however, can be that ideas are often talked through with the client, and mashed and mangled until in the end everyone agrees. We might say they find a common denominator, but this may well be the lowest common denominator. Original ideas demand the exact opposite of democracy: a determined and authoritative leader with the courage of conviction.

Client Spar European Shopping Centers GmbH | Concept Marcus Wild, Christoph Andexlinger

▲ **Strategy:** The Salzburg Europark (owned by SES) is the only shopping mall in Europe to boast its own arts centre. Named the OVAL, it offers a high-quality programme of cabaret, theatre, concerts and films, and hosts exhibitions by both international and local artists. Although this unusual idea met with some opposition initially, it has now become an integral part of the shopping centre, and of the local cultural scene.

Talking point: As a creative director, if you're not interested in new ideas, how can you expect your team to come up with anything original? If you want to know how far your team is prepared to go into unknown territory, find out whether the managing directors are behind you first!

Credits Xosé Teiga

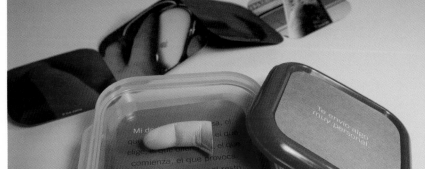

▶ **Strategy:** This provocative direct mail promotes the designer and creative Xosé Teiga: 'I'm sending you something very personal. My finger. It thinks, it creates, it beckons, it chooses, it differentiates, it begins, it does. If you want to know the rest: www.xoseteiga.com'

Talking point: What means, resources and authority must the agency give a creative director to ensure that eagerness to please takes second place to a spirit of adventure?

Client **Samsung Tesco**
Agency **CHEIL WORLDWIDE**

▼ **Strategy:** To publicize the opening of the new HomePlus supermarket, an entire underground station was papered with posters to make people think they were already in the store.

Talking point: Have you ever stopped to think what might be the positive offshoots if an unusual idea of yours became a total flop? Name at least three advantages for you personally, and then decide whether the negative consequences are so terrible that you should never risk doing something original again.

A CREATIVE DEPARTMENT IS NOT A BLACK BOX

Take a box and get a few people to put old pieces of clockwork inside it. Close the box, and give it a good shake. Then take off the lid and see if you've managed to make a working clock.

If your aim is to set up a top-flight creative department, don't make the mistake of seeing it as an isolated unit, independent of the world around it. On the contrary, it should be an open system, with information and resources flowing in at one end, and solutions coming out at the other. The quality of these will always be directly connected to the way in which your department handles the input that it receives. If the relevant in-house or out-of-house departments – sales, project management, account handling, suppliers, partner companies – don't know the rules of the game, or interfere by applying their own rules, the outcome will be a drastic lowering of standards.

Ideas are delicate creatures. Whether they survive and thrive often depends on a particular climate. That is why one of a team leaders's most basic tasks is to ensure that every co-worker and department in your agency knows how their own department functions.

In other words, you must make it clear right from the start how creativity functions, and what are the concrete requirements if it is to flourish. Otherwise, colleagues may start to think that your team is nothing more than a mysterious black box which will miraculously churn out great ideas no matter what rubbish you put in it. Your creative process should set the standards for all your partners, and if it doesn't, you will be at the mercy of outside influences instead of leading the way by dint of the talents of your fellow creatives. However, in the real world, most creative directors that fail do this for a very different reason. They themselves often don't know how the creative process can best be encouraged, and so they have difficulty communicating its needs both inside and outside the agency. That is why you should use this book to help you formulate the precepts and priorities that govern your own creative approach.

HOLD THE FLAME OF A CANDLE UP TO THE BLACK SURFACE.

NO ONE WILL KEEP US FROM SEEING

AMNESTY INTERNATIONAL

CHALLENGE:

OUR OBJECTIVE WAS TO MAKE PEOPLE UNDERSTAND THE MEANING OF THE AMNESTY CANDLE (BRING THE HORRORS TO LIGHT; NO ONE WILL KEEP US FROM SEEING) AND BOOST AMNESTY'S BRAND APPEAL.

SOLUTION:

WE CREATED AN "INTERACTIVE CARD". THE PEOPLE WHO BOUGHT THE CANDLE RECEIVED A CARD WITH IT. THEY HAD TO BRING THE FLAME OF THE CANDLE CLOSE THE THE BLACK CARD TO SEE THE IMAGE THAT WAS HIDDEN BEHIND THE BLACK SURFACE.

RESULTS:

TWICE THE AMOUNT OF CANDLES WERE SOLD (IN COMPARAISON TO THE YEAR BEFORE). THIS RESULT WAS WAY OVER OUR CLIENT'S EXPECTATONS.

AMNESTY INTERNATIONAL

◀ **Strategy:** 'Bring the horrors to light!' Amnesty International sold candles in return for donations, and each one was accompanied by a black card. When you held the candle close to the card, a hidden picture emerged, illustrating a violation of human rights.

Talking point: A leader who understands how the creative process can be harnessed will be able to inform both internal and external partners what kind of input will lead to the best results. If you don't do this, you can hardly expect your partners to do the right thing and give you the right resources purely by instinct.

▶ **Strategy:** This ad demonstrates the strength of Scott's super-absorbent kitchen towels with the aid of an optical illusion.

SUPER ABSORBENT

Scott

Talking point: Do your clients know how to engage the interest and enthusiasm of your creative team?

▲ **Strategy:** The final portfolios of some 600 students at the London College of Fashion are displayed in the form of postcards. You choose a card and put it on one of four interactive tables. Then the complete portfolio appears on the tabletop screen, and with one finger you can move, enlarge or scroll through the images.

Talking point: From time to time, invite your partners, suppliers, project managers and clients to take part in the creative process. You should only do this if you feel confident that you can steer the process in the right direction. There is no better way to convey to them what is involved in developing great ideas like the one shown above. There may even be a side benefit: they may come up with fresh and helpful ideas of their own.

NOT EVERYONE CAN BE A CREATIVE DIRECTOR

Would you hire an artist to be head of your accounts department? If not, then why would you appoint a bean-counter to be head of your creative department?

The ideal creative director is a rare breed, because the job requires a passionate creative with flair, lots of experience, the ability to think logically, strategically and analytically, and also lashings of social skills. In practice, the post frequently goes to someone who has won lots of awards at festivals, or who has gradually advanced to this position after many long years of service in the same agency. But a good creative will not necessarily be a good creative director. Here is a little test to show what attributes and skills a good creative director needs to have. If you possess at least 70 per cent of these attributes, you can regard yourself as a suitable candidate for the job.

What should you as director bring to a creative department?

▶ You should be able to cope with issues beyond the magical processes of creation: e.g. ensuring that your team's ideas stay focused on the task in hand, and using various methods and creative strategies to generate ideas.

▶ You should be a creative virtuoso yourself, offering a continuous stream of ideas rather than leaving it to chance that someone else will come up with the right goods.

▶ Your experience and talent should enable you to seize on the potential of incomplete ideas, and you should not be put off if they are unusual or if the majority of your colleagues are against them. Use your own judgment.

► Your agency should have a vision, and it is up to you to convey this to the team and inspire them with your own enthusiasm.

► If you come up against obstacles or resistance of any kind, you should see it as an exciting opportunity and accept it as a challenge, not treat it as a cause for complaint.

► As well as being a creative, you must be a judge and an enabler. You should be able to be an optimist at one moment and a pessimist the next, because you need to be fully aware of the positive and negative sides of an idea, so that you can weigh them up against each other in order to form a balanced judgment.

► You should not approach projects with a feeling of hesitancy or indecision. If the situation demands it, you need to be able to make a swift and firm decision.

► You should have an unerring instinct for spotting talent, and you should have the social skills to encourage and promote it.

► You should have demonstrated through previous projects that you can overcome all obstacles and stick to your guns right through to a successful outcome.

► You should be passionate about your work and seek out colleagues who will share your passion, who will inspire and be inspired by you.

► You should not only have an instinct for good ideas, but also be interested only in the very best. There can be no compromise on quality for you.

► You should have the ability to work with different people of different characters and interests, so that every member of the team will try to scale the same heights as you.

► You should encourage a culture in which mistakes are allowed, and you should overcome setbacks in such a way that your team members will learn from their mistakes and even turn them to their advantage.

► You should be flexible, and should not cling to past glories. You should encourage your team to break away from tired routines and outdated practices, and to keep trying new things.

► You should inspire trust and confidence, and come down hard on intrigue and back-biting.

► You should not allow your department to become a ghetto, and ensure that it always remains open to ideas from outside.

► Whether you're dealing with clients or your own agency, you should present your team's ideas with total commitment and conviction, so that everyone will share your enthusiasm.

► You should have the courage to take responsibility, and not blame any errors on your team.

► You should be a charismatic leader, having earned the trust and the loyalty of your team.

► You should be a great manager, able to delegate particular tasks to the right people, and to deal systematically and efficiently with routine administrative matters.

► You should be able to see the wider context of every project, and deal with the business side of your job as enthusiastically as you deal with the more creative side.

THE CREATIVE DIRECTOR AS TEAM COACH

Attending a creative meeting doesn't automatically make you a creative – just as you don't become a footballer by simply stepping onto the pitch.

Leading a creative team means knowing the rules and getting your players to give their best in every game. It's not a matter of coming up with your own ideas every time, but of nurturing other people's talents and making sure the team gels. Enthusiasm, productive meetings, openness to new ideas, persistence, helpful guidance from start to finish – these are the hallmarks of a good leader. You must be the team coach, and this entails knowledge that goes far beyond your own intuitive creative gifts. But there will no doubt come a time when you must decide whether you're going to be a player-manager, or simply a manager. I've known creative directors who actually compete with their own team members in the field of ideas, and this raises the whole question of whether a top-class player is the ideal person to coach the rest of the side. It can happen that the biggest stars on the field are the worst communicators off it. Really great directors will show their true class by asking along people who are even more competent than themselves in some areas. They may be more inventive, or better at photography or graphic design, but the crucial thing for you to keep in mind is that you don't have to be better than everyone else at everything.

Client **Print it!** | Creatives **Maria de Ros Padrós, architect/Daniel Loewe, photographer**

▲ Strategy: A signage system to guide visitors around an exhibition.

Talking point: As team coach, the creative director needs to set up a framework within which creatives can experiment without constantly wondering how the whole system works. They can concentrate entirely on their own field, instead of wasting a third of their time and energy trying to find out what they can and can't do.

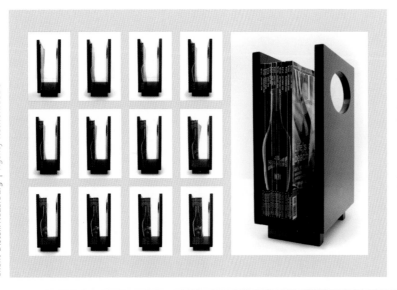

Client Distell/Nederburg | Agency Network BBDO

◀ **Strategy:** Fine wine needs time to mature. To illustrate this fact, an ad was placed on the spine of twelve issues of a wine magazine. By the end of the year, the image of the bottle was complete.

Talking point: Chuck Daley, former coach of the Detroit Pistons, once said of the NBA: 'It's a players' league. They allow you to coach them or they don't. Once they stop allowing you to coach, you're on your way out.' It's a similar situation with creative teams and their directors. What influence does the team coach have on innovative ideas like this one?

▶ **Strategy:** A single-page ad in *The Times of India* caused such a sensation that within a short time the whole of India was engaged in a movement for political and social reform. A few months later, the ad developed into a nationwide direct response campaign involving TV, the press, the internet, mobiles and reality TV. The 'DO!' campaign gathered committed support from actors, writers, musicians, politicians, activists and industrialists all over India.

Talking point: Are you satisfied if you have led your team to the point where they have come up with a great idea, or do you wish you'd come up with it yourself?

THE TIMES OF INDIA

A PASSAGE FROM INDIA | P 2   THE GOOD, THE BAD & TOI'S RATING METER | P 12-15

India v/s India

There are two Indias in this country.

One India is straining at the leash, eager to spring forth and live up to all the adjectives that the world has been showering recently upon us.

The other India is the leash.

One India says, give me a chance and I'll prove myself. The other India says, prove yourself first and maybe then you'll have a chance.

One India lives in the optimism of our hearts. The other India lurks in the skepticism of our minds.

**One India wants. The other India hopes.
One India leads. The other India follows.**

But conversions are on the rise. With each passing day more and more people from the other India have been coming over to this side. And quietly, while the world is not looking, a pulsating, dynamic, new India is emerging.

An India whose faith in success is far greater than its fear of failure. An India that no longer boycotts foreign-made goods but buys out the companies that make them instead.

History, they say, is a bad motorist. It rarely ever signals its intentions when it is taking a turn.

This is that rarely-ever moment. History is turning a page.

For more than half a century, our nation has sprung, stumbled, run, fallen, rolled over, got up, dusted herself and cantered, sometimes lurched on. But today, as we begin our 60th year as a free nation, the ride has brought us to the edge of time's great precipice.

And one India - a tiny little voice at the back of the head - is looking down at the bottom of the ravine and hesitating.

The other India is looking up at the sky and saying, it's time to fly.

THE TIMES OF INDIA

Client *The Times of India* | Agency JWT

WHO IS RESPONSIBLE FOR WHAT?

Imagine that you can do anything within your creative team except take the really important decisions. In many agencies, there's actually a name for this role: Creative Director!

In my experience, some companies employ a creative director *and* someone else who takes all the important creative decisions. In extreme cases, the creative director officially bears all the responsibility, while the unofficial creative director has the last word when it comes to matters of selection or presentation. The unofficial director remains in the background, and is often a board member. The project leader, or someone from the client's side of the project, may assume the role. This very common mishmash of responsibilities can involve several people with a variety of titles. Ultimately, it comes down to a single question: why does this particular agency employ a creative director? If the agency doesn't trust the person concerned to fulfil their designated role, the two might as well part company. The effect of this type of situation on the rest of the team and its work can be devastating. If it's not clear who is responsible for what, there can be no outcome but uncertainty and frustration, followed by an inevitable descent into mediocrity because everyone will be too scared to try anything different. Real leadership means having the unequivocal right to make decisions and tackle tasks and problems head-on. The title that you give to this person is immaterial, so long as the role, the responsibility and the authority are made clear to everyone.

▼ **Strategy:** Bags made
from real crocodile skin.

Genuine crocodile leather bag.

Suzusen

Client **Suzusen** | Agency **Grey**

Talking point: Let's assume that we need to make a decision: we must choose an idea
for a campaign and approve it for implementation. In your agency, who makes this
kind of decision – one person, or a committee? How much authority does the creative
director have if the decision is normally made by several people?

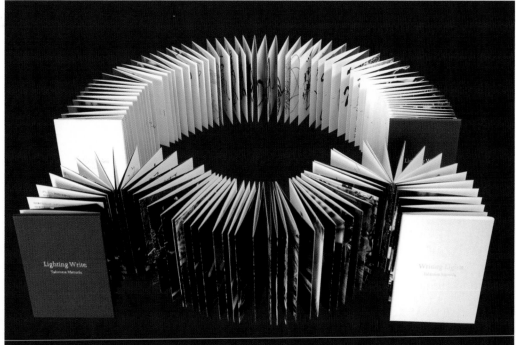

◀ **Strategy:** Fan-fold brochure for the Kawasaki City Museum.

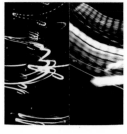

Talking point: If it's not clear who is responsible for what in your team, original ideas like this one may never get a chance, because no one will dare to greenlight them.

◀ **Strategy:** The goal of this campaign was to draw attention to the launch of a Dutch TV reality gameshow, *The Phone*. Mobile phones were concealed during some popular radio and TV programmes, and at any time or place the characteristic ringtone would sound. If someone picked up the phone, a voiceover would announce that the new season of the gameshow had begun.

Talking point: A weak chain of command can often lead to uncertainty about who is responsible for what. Check whether your colleagues are actually doing the roles that have been designated to them.

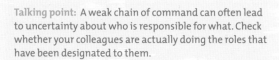

SHAKE UP THE DESIRE FOR SECURITY

Perhaps creative directors should start behaving like presidents and step down after a certain number of years. This would give a boost to those who want creativity, and a slap in the face to those who only want job security.

Most people strive for stability and security. Any change or innovation is regarded as a threat and therefore meets with resistance. In my experience, the most flagrant example of this is to be found in the TV industry. The more the programme-makers focus on their own job security, the less open they are to new ideas. Their thoughts and actions are governed by the need to play safe, and that means sticking with tried and trusted formulas. These people generally go through three phases: first, they come up with their own successes; next they consolidate and expand on these successes; and finally they barricade themselves and their successes and their position in the company behind a brick wall and fight off any attempt to bring in change. This is the point at which creativity reaches rock bottom.

If you also look at personal backgrounds, you may discern another factor that helps to entrench the status quo: most of these people are over forty, and as well as their career they also have to think of their luxury car, expensive holidays, the demands of their family, their mortgage, their pension and all the other status symbols that a star performer needs. They have

a great deal to lose – far too much for them to risk everything on an unpredictable, untried experiment.

The fact of the matter is, however, that TV producers and planners are not paid to repeat the successes of yesteryear; their task is – or should be – to initiate the bold ideas that will lead to the successes of the future. And so the question arises as to how to achieve a balance between the need for stability and the insecurity inevitably engendered by risk and change. I don't think there is any magical solution, but perhaps those in charge simply need to make themselves more open to unconventional ideas. One possibility might be give key decision-makers a fixed term in office. A limited tenure would make it pointless for people to try to institutionalize their former successes, and of course they would be unable to secure their positions by resisting change. By fixing the term of leadership posts, and combining this with a culture in which risks can be taken and mistakes made, you may well create a far more fertile climate for originality. Perhaps all companies need to work out for themselves how they can best prevent their creative teams from turning into mere administrators.

► **Strategy:** The Axe website *The Fixer Show* takes the form of a multi-episode chat show that promises to solve all your problems with the help of a wisecracking presenter and a few scantily clad girls.

Client Unilever | Agency Mekanism

Talking point: Supposing you were to redefine the concept of success for directors? Two failures a year might be an acceptable indication of inventiveness and hence of future success.

► **Strategy:** *Weeds* is a Golden Globe-winning US comedy-drama series. To sell advertising slots during its third season, hemp plants were packaged to look like oversized joints and sent out as bouquets to press and media agencies.

Client TV6 | Agency Le Bureau

Talking point: What effect would it have on your agency's approach if the directors offered rewards for innovation and risk-taking?

'How can you stop yourself from going mad? I don't mean the madness that creates crazy ideas inside agencies, but the madness of the real world outside which sometimes paralyses creativity inside.'

Source unknown

CREATIVE TEAM LEADING

Clients and creatives come from two different worlds, and in many areas they follow two different sets of rules. That is why a project in its initial stages needs some kind of interpreter or referee to translate, filter and facilitate communications between the two parties. One of the tasks of the creative director is to make sure that clients aren't so confused by the various ideas that they start to think they're dealing with a load of unhinged artists. For their part, the creative team may be equally horrified by the prospect of crazy clients swamping them with their own nightmarish demands: the endless pressure of deadlines, evaluations, expectations, the real world, the imperative need for success. The creative director must stand at the head of the troops, protecting them and ensuring that nothing penetrates the inner circle except what is good for the team and for the project. Endless criticism and unyielding pressure rarely lead to success. And so for the sake of both parties, the creative director must play the key role of go-between, smoothing out any differences with tact, diplomacy and, if necessary, a bit of discreet censorship. Project managers or account handlers should only take on this role if they know exactly what makes the creative team tick, and understand exactly what is meant by idea management.

HARVEY NICHOLS SALE
KNIGHTSBRIDGE · LONDON

HARVEY NICHOLS SALE
KNIGHTSBRIDGE · LONDON

▲ Strategy: This print campaign shows what a Harvey Nichols sale can turn people into.

Talking point: Do you know what external influences might encourage your team to develop ideas like this one, and what might inhibit them?

Client **Nestlé Peters** | Agency **Publicis Mojo**

◀ Strategy: Larger-than-life statues acted as a reminder to Australians that Frosty Fruits are a delicious way to cool down as summer gets underway. A radio campaign invited the people of Sydney to take photos of themselves with the statues and take part in a prize draw.

Talking point: Many talented teams develop a private little world with their own language and in-jokes that no one from outside can possibly understand. Inside this sheltered microclimate, extraordinary ideas can flourish more easily than in departments that are permanently exposed to negative influences.

IDEAS CAN PUT YOU IN A MINORITY OF ONE

*'If you follow the herd,
you end up as a steak.'*

Source unknown

If you come up with a radical new idea, you will be on your own at first. There are some people who may be uncomfortable at this thought, simply because they feel more secure within a group. They do everything they can to fit in and earn the recognition of their colleagues. If creative directors do this, however, there is a danger that they will fail to give adequate support to original ideas, and will begin to give in at the slightest opposition. Top creative directors that I know personally are able to live with being outsiders, and in fact they often enjoy it. They have long since learned how to cope with the risk of not being taken seriously or of being subjected to fierce criticism. These are people who are prepared to follow their own instincts and not only to welcome originality but also to defend it if need be, even against the wishes of the majority. For them, deviating from the norm can actually be fun, and they feel it gives them the chance to make their mark on the world. From this point of view, creative directors may have the loneliest job in the world, because in addition to embracing controversy and criticism, they must also be committed enough to take responsibility for all the consequences, whether positive or negative.

Client **Venti Eventi** | Creative **Jan Vormann**

◄ Strategy: *Dispatchwork* was an installation in the Italian town of Bocchignano, as part of the group project '20 Eventi'. Damaged walls were repaired with pieces of Lego.

Talking point: Do your directors encourage eccentric projects like this, or do they prefer to retreat into their conventional shells?

► Strategy: At Christmas time in New York, Charmin Toilet Tissues set up pop-up restrooms to provide for the needs of New Yorkers and tourists alike. There was a choice of 20 luxurious lavatories, and each one was cleaned after use.

Client **Procter & Gamble** | Agency **Gigunda Group, Inc.**

Talking point: What guarantees would a creative director require before promoting a revolutionary new idea that ran contrary to current trends?

LURE YOUR TEAM TO CREATIVE DESTRUCTION

Are you thinking of nothing but the benefits of your client's product? Then you're ignoring half of the potential opportunities to develop original ideas.

One of the creative director's most important duties is to know when to set the team free. The best example you can set is to show no hesitation when it comes to presenting a product from a perspective that the client would be extremely reluctant to endorse. Be radical. Make fun of the product, smash it up, look for its weaknesses, tear it to pieces, or look for ways in which it could be used to hurt people. In many cases, negatives offer the best chances of creative originality, because they always show a new and unexpected angle compared to hackneyed and conventional viewpoints. Of course the object is not to damage the product's reputation, but simply to surprise and delight the viewer with something radically different.

By attacking the product, you can sometimes draw attention to values and benefits that no one had previously noticed. The negative approach opens new doors, and a creative director should have the courage to do just this. Tempt your team. Show them how much you enjoy a bout of childish chaos – what fun it can be to smash a few icons, undermine authority, and question things that people take for granted. You are the one who has to make this spark ignite, but if you umm and err, don't expect your team to start whooping with enthusiasm. If all you and your team can do is come up with the same old superlatives, the outcome will be a mass of boring clichés and ultimately the deadest of dead ends.

◄ Strategy: This Gahns® print campaign suggests the trouble you might get into if your soap is not on a rope.

Gahns®
Soap on a rope

Talking point: If the creative director is a stick-in-the-mud, how can the team pull itself out of the mire?

► Strategy: Coke ZERO's table football lets three teams play against each other.

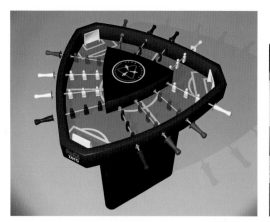 

Talking point: Creative destruction means taking something apart and then putting it back together again in an original way. Leaving existing conventions untouched and simply hoping that something new will emerge is never a fruitful approach.

▲ Strategy: This print campaign provides an exaggerated illustration of just how sour Marbels candy really is.

Talking point: The creative director should encourage the team to make fun of products, projects, and even clients. By focusing on their negative side, you can release a whole new range of original ideas.

'*Our creatives are far too busy to burn out.*
That kind of thing only happens to people
who haven't got enough to do!'

Head of an agency network

One of the most neglected causes of creative burnout is exhaustion. If you spend 14 hours a day, six days a week, giving your all, it won't be long before you end up in a disastrous cul-de-sac of tiredness, numbness and apathy. Burnout can also come through frustration – failure to reach unreasonable targets, or your own excessively high demands on yourself, or the constant pressure of deadlines. For creative directors who aim to keep their team right at the top, there is a simple prescription: if you want the best, take a rest. There needs to be a balance between dynamic motivation and restorative relaxation – in the correct dose, a tonic can revive you; in the wrong dose, it can poison you. I'd now like to suggest two ways in which an agency with the best intentions can inspire its team to hit the heights, but at the same time risk bringing it down to the lowest depths through overkill. Some firms give their creative departments the freedom to design their workplace exactly as they want it. As a result, the creatives often

feel more at home there than they do in the rented accommodation which is all they can afford. A lot of them only go home to sleep, and they have no private lives to speak of. The second strategy – again usually implemented with the best intentions – is for the office, data and equipment to be permanently available, and for working hours to be totally flexible, because this kind of freedom engenders a sense of personal responsibility and commitment. The result is that people go on working on their projects even in private, so that to all intents and purposes the dividing line between work and leisure is obliterated. Basically, these modern working methods seem to make very good sense, and they may also be effective. However, this will only be the case if self-motivation doesn't spill over into a destructive form of self-exploitation. In this situation, it is the director's responsibility to look after the welfare of the team and, if necessary, to take an individual on one side and insist on a break, with a view to helping that person strike the right balance between work and play. If the director doesn't intervene in time, exhaustion will lead to all the frustrations listed above, even to illnesses and ultimately resignation. But sadly, it can often happen that directors will merely shrug their shoulders and move on, because there are always young and enthusiastic talents knocking on the door, only too eager to step into the same trap.

▼ **Strategy:** Stage set for the Rolling Stones' 'A Bigger Bang' world tour.

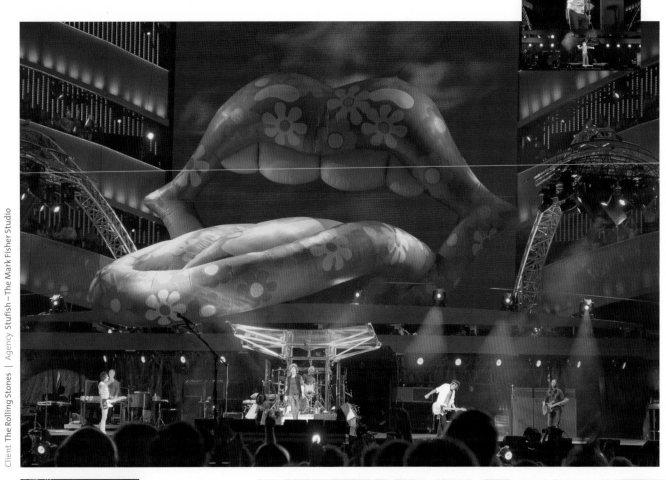

Client The Rolling Stones | Agency Stufish – The Mark Fisher Studio

Talking point: Let's assume that your team begins each month with 100 per cent energy and motivation, and this is only regenerated by the requisite number of breaks. What do you think would be the ideal working method to extract the best possible results from them? In percentage terms, what energy level do you think your team members are working on at present?

▲ Strategy: The ski manufacturers K2 created a trade fair stand in the style of a Caribbean island, complete with skull and crossbones.

Talking point: Teams that are constantly working flat out will eventually run out of steam. When was the last time your team had fun coming up with a batch of original ideas like this one?

◄ Strategy: The Diesel Liquid Space fashion show took the form of a dazzling multimedia spectacle, making use of holographic projections of computer-generated sea creatures.

Client **Diesel** | Agency **Dvein/Vizoo**

Talking point: How do the members of your team recharge their batteries? How high is personnel turnover, and are changes caused by loss of interest or burnout?

RECOGNITION IS THE BEST REWARD

Demotivational Rule No. 1: treat your creatives like sheltered artists. Never offer them any information, give them nothing but negative feedback, and always keep them away from the client.

Some people work just so that they can earn enough to do what they want in their private lives. Others are totally committed to their job, and that is what gives them satisfaction. Many directors seem unaware of the fact that almost all designers, writers, editors, event managers, photographers and illustrators belong to the second category. A director who is incapable of handing out plaudits, recognizing talent, or who regards colleagues as competitors, hasn't a clue about the job. And yet the creative industries are often devoid of all human warmth, because as often as not, the creatives themselves feel unloved. For them, recognition is the most important reward – how else can you explain the enthusiasm and com-

mitment of people who are so badly paid? So massage their egos, give them positive feedback, make them feel wanted. Creative team leading means a great deal more than trying to be cool. For instance, if your team are working on a campaign for a major sporting event, make sure they get a chance to go into the VIP lounge, maybe to appear in an ad, take home some of the props, even hobnob with the stars and attend the launch presentations. Nothing will inspire them more than this kind of recognition. But sadly and all too frequently, it's the bosses who grab the glory: they get themselves invited to all the parties, leaving the real heroes back in their studios, slaving away on the next project in line.

◄ **Strategy:** The Wishing Tree was a Christmas promotion for the citizens of Madrid. With the help of 21 helpers dressed as elves, people wrote wishes on helium-filled balloons that were eventually released into the sky from the 32-metre tower. Some 100,000 people took part and the final ceremony was attended by a crowd of 40,000 spectators.

Talking point: Creatives who are involved in a really fascinating project think less about money and far more about the fact that they are doing something original which will stay in people's memories for a long time to come. What sort of projects can you envisage that would be a reward in themselves?

CREATIVE TEAMS

03

Surely some of the brightest stars in the creative firmament would want to work in your team? All you have to do is find out what you've done to stop them.

The above may seem a little far-fetched, but it's well worth thinking about. Even if you wouldn't actually want the top stars in your team, at least think about the implications. If you're honest with yourself, you may learn quite a lot about your team, your clients, your creative culture and attitude towards ideas, and last but not least, yourself. It may surprise you to find out that the reasons why high-fliers flock to particular agencies are quite different from those you might have expected. Do you think it's all about cool projects, stylish offices, impressive job titles, enviable salaries – or could the attraction be something else that is even more motivating? You can probably answer part of this question yourself, but the rest might best be discussed directly with your colleagues. That, however, is the subject of this chapter. I want to get you thinking differently about creative teams, and experimenting with alternative structures within your department.

Andy Bird

Chris Bangle

Dan Wieden

Dave Bowman

Matthias Eickmeyer

John Condon

John Moore

Nick Worthington

Lars Bastholm

Marcello Serpa

Neil Huxley

Stefan Sagmeister

Pat Fallon

Sean Mullens

Ruth Jonsara

Credits Talpa Content B.V. | Photo Roy Beusker

▼ Strategy: In the gameshow *I Love My Country*, two teams of celebrities answer questions on topics like music, sport, culture and history, to show how much they know about their homeland. Each team gets plenty of support from its fans in the audience. Devised by Dutch TV producers Endemol, this successful format has already been sold to eight different countries.

Talking point: Imagine that the world's best independent consultants have made a detailed inspection of your agency and now want to translate their findings into three concrete changes. What do you think these would be, if the aim is to attract the most talented creatives in the country?

I'm often asked what motivates creative teams to keep coming up with great ideas. Basically, there's one simple formula: put a permanent stop to demotivation!

I know that creatives are usually highly motivated by their love of good ideas, and frankly it's quite simple to keep this passion burning: just remove anything and everything that might quench it. But in my experience, some agencies go out of their way to discover ways of stifling enthusiasm. Here are three top tips on how to put out the creative fire:

1. Leave your team totally in the dark about what your goal is. Force them to keep going back to the drawing board, so that they look like idiots who haven't got a clue what they're doing.

2. At any meeting (or brainstorming session), mix up idea development, implementation and sheer fantasy as confusingly as possible. While some of your colleagues are trying to put forward new ideas, others will be talking about how impractical they are, because they'll be thinking of the end while the first lot are thinking of the beginning. An excellent strategy.

3. Make sure your team gets far more criticism than praise, and withhold vital information from them. This will show them how important you are, and how unimportant they are.

Of course I realize that there are no limits to these techniques, and there are lots more ways of crushing your subordinates. In this kind of context, there is little point in developing meaningful ways of boosting motivation until you can put a stop to this self-destructive approach. Too many firms have come up with their own repertoire of morale-crushers, and so let's try to dismantle them and find an efficient way out of the bottleneck.

▶ **Strategy:** Creative spaces in the Ogilvy & Mather agency in Guangzhou, China.

Talking point: How can the immediate working environment help prevent a creative team from getting bogged down in a routine that could undermine their natural enthusiasm?

Client Forus | Agency Prolam Y&R

EL AIRE QUE ENFRIA TU HOGAR

CALIENTA EL MUNDO
STOP GLOBAL WARMING

◆ Columbia

◀ Strategy: 'The air that cools your home is heating up the world. Stop global warming.'

Talking point: The moment people stop having fun with their own creativity, they start to repeat themselves and reject original ideas like the one above. They take the path of least resistance, hoping to avoid further frustration.

▶ Strategy: Puma's new collection 'Pumus Trendycus' was unveiled to a captive audience in the puma enclosure at Zagreb Zoo.

Talking point: Think of two concrete measures you could adopt in order to get your team thinking along lines as original as this.

Client Puma | Agency Bruketa & Zinic OM

ANYONE CAN BE CREATIVE

The creative industries have an interesting issue: no one really knows how to encourage or channel creativity. Consequently, creative teams don't like putting their cards on the table. They prefer to maintain a mystique about their work, and cling to the belief that creatives like themselves are the only people who ever have ideas.

Absolutely anyone can take part in the idea development phase. Later, when theory has to be put into practice, you need professionals with skills that guarantee the best possible implementation. In other words, a passer-by in the street can come up with an idea, but you need the best photographers, designers, illustrators, camera operators or animators to make it real and make it good. So don't hesitate to invite outsiders to join the team at the beginning, because they can bring fresh energy. And you don't need to look too far afield – there are probably lots of departments in your agency and your client's company, and all of them will bring their own particular experiences and expertise to the project. In future, draw a line between the ideas phase, which is open to all, and the implementation phase, which requires specialist skills.

Credits From a TV ad for Centraal Beheer | Illustrator Max Julian Otto

▲ **Strategy:** Two men have an appointment at the airport. It's clearly the first time they've ever met, and they cordially shake hands. They then go straight to a glider, climb aboard and give the signal to start. When they are airborne, two more men meet and shake hands. At that moment they hear the glider's towrope snap with a loud crack above them, and they look up in surprise. They turn around, and we suddenly see that the word 'instructor' is written on both their jackets. Their astonishment makes it clear that the two guys in the glider are meant to be their pupils. This TV ad was made for the insurance company Centraal Beheer.

Talking point: We all know of real-life stories that are so strange, shocking or ridiculous that they're difficult to believe. Do you know any people whose store of knowledge and experience could enrich the creativity of your team?

▶ **Strategy:** Heineken was the official beer of the Austin City Limits music festival, which meant that the local Spoetzl brewery couldn't sell its Shiner beer there. Spoetzl reacted by mounting a two-phase campaign. First, on all three days visitors to the festival were greeted in the car park by posters bearing various messages. Next, thousands of labels were handed out to the public outside the festival site. These were designed to fit perfectly around the Heineken cans and give the impression that people were actually drinking Shiner.

Client Spoetzl Brewery | Agency McGarrah Jessee

Talking point: This sort of idea might come to anyone, including visitors to the festival or brewery workers and their friends. How can you make your team members willing to embrace ideas from outsiders?

IS YOUR TEAM READY TO EMBRACE THE STRANGE?

If you want creativity, you need to heat up the competition for ideas. The more varied the knowledge, personalities and qualifications of your team members, the more interesting will be the results. The best raw material for new ideas is knowledge from all spheres of life.

If your team works in product design, for instance, you can provide them with a huge amount of stimulus by inviting outsiders from, say, the fashion world or architecture to join the group. These outsiders can broaden horizons simply because they think differently, know different things, and look at the world through different perspectives. However, I'd like to go one step further and suggest you should even invite an eccentric or two, just in order to stir things up a bit. The fact that this suggestion is not crazy in itself can be proved by some of the top agency creatives, who for all their eccentricity have proved themselves over and over again, because they have minds of their own and are also incredibly motivated. You will see from their CVs that most of them have not come up via the conventional training and career path. That is precisely why they are potentially capable of breaking all the rules, applying different areas of knowledge, and following their own instincts.

The perception that eccentric outsiders can act as a stimulus to the creativity of the team has become quite commonplace, but in practice it rarely happens. This is due to an almost paradoxical reaction by the team itself: they will do everything they can to make 'deviants' conform to the existing system. If they won't conform, both they and their work will come under attack, with the end result that their ideas are either ridiculed or shoved into someone's drawer to gather dust. The same phenomenon can be observed in marketing departments, conservative design studios, and international TV companies. If you are thinking of bringing in an outsider with crazy ideas and an unconventional approach, make sure that you and your team are properly prepared. Let the newcomer feel that innovative suggestions have at least a chance of survival. At the same time, you should aim to integrate outsiders in such a way that they can pursue their own path while at the same time feeling that they're still part of the team. People who are deliberately ostracized by the majority will almost inevitably find that their ideas are soon discarded by the insiders.

Credits Theo Jansen

▶ **Strategy:** For nearly twenty years, Theo Jansen has been creating kinetic sculptures, which he calls Strandbeests ('Beach Beasts'). They are made from plastic tubes, cables, nylon string and sticky tape. They move spontaneously in the wind, and according to the artist, they are meant to evolve gradually into autonomous living beings. These 'beasts' are able to anchor themselves in the sand when there is an approaching storm, and their antennae can sense obstacles and enable them to change direction when they come into contact with the water.

Talking point: Invite extraordinary people to team meetings, and let them bring new meanings to ordinary objects and situations.

Credits Juan Mann

◀ **Strategy:** In 2004, Juan Mann began offering 'Free Hugs' in Pitt Street Mall, Sydney. He carried a placard and waited for passers-by to approach him. Initially his offer was greeted with some scepticism, but eventually the idea took on something of a cult following. Shimon Moore, lead singer of the Australian band Sick Puppies, produced a video of Mann, recording the early stages of the campaign, how it spread, an attempt by the police to ban it, and the collection of signatures backing Mann. The video created a big stir on YouTube and was seen by over 50 million people. This resulted in a worldwide Free Hugs movement.

Talking point: If you decide to include an outsider in the team for a particular project, make sure that their field of expertise is as distant as possible from the one you are dealing with. The looser the connection, the more exciting the results will be.

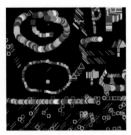

▶ **Strategy:** The popular iPhone app Doodle Kids was designed and programmed by nine-year-old Lim Ding Wen from Singapore. It's a drawing app for children, and offers a huge range of shapes and colours.

Talking point: Has it ever occurred to you and your team to ask for ideas from people who don't know the first thing about the subject you're tackling? Why not ask some children to tackle a particular problem you're grappling with?

TRIBES AND COMMUNITIES

While your team is struggling to find a solution, there may be little groups of people in playgrounds, pubs or internet forums who are already putting into practice amazing ideas the team would never have thought of.

If your creative team is genuinely on the look-out for good ideas, they should be ready to go on the occasional trip to another world. For instance, out to the edges of our society, where small groups get together in order to work on wild and crazy projects that don't even have a proper name. For instance, they might be raiding a scrapyard to pick up perfectly ordinary materials like pipes, planks, wires and brackets, wanting to convert them into new furniture designs. Successful products can be the fruit of passionate internet discussions or spring from clubs and institutions. What connects all these people is a certain dissatisfaction with the status quo, or an irresistible desire simply to do something different. For instance, you might see young people riding specially modified unicycles through the town in a weird kind of obstacle race, and they'll take it as seriously as a Grand Prix because they have great pride in their skills. Over the

designated course, they must find the most elegant way of crossing obstacles to a musical accompaniment. This is just one example of people with shared values and interests coming together to indulge in activities that much of contemporary society has neither space nor time for. These so-called tribes band together in socially deprived areas, on the internet, in private clubs or on sports fields. What they all share is the need to exchange ideas with like-minded folk, and be recognized for what they've achieved. This kind of motivation opens up the way for a new form of cooperation: why not invite tribes and outsider groups to join you on a particular project, because they might have spent years focusing on particular themes and developing expertise that you won't find anywhere else. Ask yourself what unfamiliar perspectives, skills or flights of fancy could inspire your team to reach new heights.

Credits Estudio enPieza

◄ **Strategy:** A lamp made out of dozens of BIC ballpoint pens.

▼ **Strategy:** A lamp made out of old neon tubes.

Credits Castor

Talking point: Look for people whose special interests or personal situations have forced them to link up with like-minded folk, so that they can go ahead and do their own thing.

Credits The Buried Life

◄ **Strategy:** In 2006, four student friends made a list of a hundred things they simply had to do before they died. They recorded their adventures on camera in the form of a documentary. Now *The Buried Life* has been turned into an MTV reality show. There is one difference in focus, however. When the four stop their bus in a particular place, they also help local people to fulfil their own dreams. For instance, they took eight sick children on a shopping spree to Toys-R-Us.

Talking point: Isn't it strange that agency creatives can devote vast amounts of time and energy to developing ideas for a particular project, while children's groups, internet forums, clubs, self-help groups and circles of friends somehow manage pretty well without professional help? How can your team find all these different talents before someone else snaps them up?

THE INTERNET IS A GOLDMINE FOR RAW IDEAS

You could have several thousand highly motivated people supplying ideas to your creative department without ever meeting any of them in person.

The internet has introduced new trends such as crowdsourcing, open innovation and mass collaboration, all of which are linked by one basic concept: independently of time and place, people from all over the world can work either with or against each other to tackle a particular problem. But what individuals from all sorts of fields perceive as a unique opportunity, the big boys of the creative industries often successfully manage to ignore. Many agencies cling on grimly to the belief that ideas are the province of their own creatives and nobody else. More fool them. An increasing number of client firms are now using the internet as an inexhaustible source of designs, product concepts and names, slogans and advertising campaigns – all supplied by volunteers from here, there and everywhere. Clients nowadays often hire the big agencies simply to implement their own ideas. If you don't want to miss out, you should position yourself and all your talents halfway between these individual networking geniuses and your clients. What you should never forget amid all this euphoric activity is that agencies still have something that collaborative projects don't have: namely, the ability to transform an initial idea into a top-quality reality. The thousands of ideas generated spontaneously on the web are of no use without professionals to select and implement them. The strength of the agencies lies in their ability to fit the ideas to the projects, to pay for expertise, to motivate experts, to choose the right concept out of the thousands on offer, to devise strategies that will transform raw material into a finished product, and of course to provide a creative director who will ensure that the right ideas are given the right form to create the right impact. In future, agencies themselves need to embrace techniques such as crowdsourcing and mass collaboration, in order to guarantee that they will get the optimal results for their clients.

Here are four ways in which you can use the web as a resource and dramatically increase the creative input you receive:

▶ **Online idea searches.** Just like a TV talent show, you can take part in a worldwide casting session for ideas and check out what's out there. The winner can be given an attractive prize and also invited to work on the implementation of the project. It is useful to begin with a brief for tasks such as design projects, product names, events or development of TV formats.

▶ **Online idea development.** For instance, a design agency might publish its preliminary concepts for a new container or piece of furniture and invite comments from outside. Professionals from all over the world then have the chance to share their thoughts, point out mistakes, suggest improvements – all of which involves other interested parties working in real time. Fields that are particularly suited to this approach are packaging, new uses of materials, product development, computer games, or screenplay ideas.

▶ **Online innovations for clients.** Dissatisfied clients or people with original ideas of their own can try their hand at turning their visions into reality. They can modify or improve their new sneaker design, make their own ad for it, design their own packaging. This is a great way of generating new concepts and products, services, packaging, events or ideas for exhibitions.

▶ **Online networking.** For particularly ambitious projects, you can bring together leading experts from all over the world in advertising, design, music, film or art. This team can work together to create original fashion shows, TV series, shopping malls or trade stands.

The internet is becoming an ever greater influence on the democratization of creativity. You can find professional-standard tools to download and use at home, and there are plenty of gifted amateurs who are well able to compete with their professional counterparts. Whether their hobby is digital photography, computer animation, music, video editing or illustration, people everywhere are experimenting, producing their own work, and putting it on the web so everyone can see it. Maybe more than 90 per cent of it would fail to meet professional standards, but that doesn't matter to its creators because they're under no economic pressure and they're not restricted by a client's requirements. With all the time and freedom they need, they can play around with ideas in a manner that is simply not possible for professional agencies. However, many creatives have now cottoned on to the fact that they can break out of their rut by systematically searching the web, selecting and refining the ideas they find there, and eventually passing them off as their own!

► **Strategy:** The neural network of our brain (on the left) and the World Wide Web (on the right) not only look similar, but also in part follow the same organizational principles. The computer scientist Francis Heylighen regards the internet as a 'Global Brain' – a superbrain that will eventually evolve into a collective intelligence.

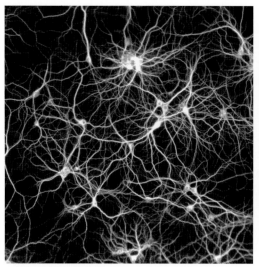

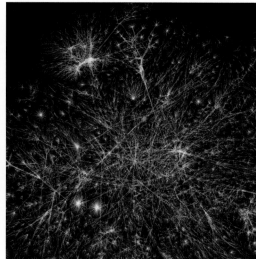

Credits **Paul De Koninck, www.greenspine.ca**

Credits **Matt Britt/Barrett Lyon**

▼ **Strategy:** What will cars look like in the future? In their quest for the answer, Audi's designers offered the internet community the chance to develop their own visions. The SPORE competition gave people six weeks to post their own designs on a special website. The technology used to render these futuristic cars was provided by the Electronic Arts (EA) game *SPORE*.

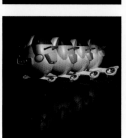

Talking point: The weight of expectation on crowdsourcing and collaborative projects is high, sometimes too high. Most websites and platforms lack certain basic features that will motivate people: the chance to take part in an exciting project, a topic relevant to themselves, a clear goal, love, personal use, and recognition. So long as platforms are unable to offer value and emotional engagement of this kind, they will rarely come up with usable results.

A THIRD OF YOUR TEAM SHOULD BE THE BEST IN THE BUSINESS

It's been said that if you don't have a horse, you can't run in the Derby. That much is pretty obvious. But if you want to win, you also need to be careful which horses you enter for the race.

There are some mean-spirited people who maintain that mediocre creatives always make for mediocre teams who end up with mediocre results. Ed Michael, director of McKinsey USA, coined the term 'the War for Talents', which makes the point that in many fields, success depends solely on getting the most highly skilled people to work for you. Nowhere is this more apparent than in the creative industries. Here everything revolves round artistic talent, practical skills, and a large slice of intuition. It may not be necessary for your team to consist exclusively of geniuses, but a third of them should be among the best in the field.

These are the 'draught horses' whose pulling power will carry the whole team along with them. It's a phenomenon that can be seen most clearly in team sports like football, where the presence of two or three international superstars can raise the entire team to new heights. Try to gather these top talents around you, because it'll be an investment that cannot fail to pay dividends. A great team develops its own special aura, which will attract more talent and guarantee results, which in turn will bring in the sort of clients you want. Don't forget, your field depends on people, and your success depends on finding the best.

► **Strategy:** The packaging for WB&CO Organic Vegetable Juice shows off the natural colours of the juices. The containers are also 100 per cent reusable and recyclable.

Client WB&CO Organic Vegetable Juice
Agency SEED Creative Consultants

Talking point: Is your creative department set up in a way that allows the top talents to raise the rest to their own level? Or are circumstances such that the stars are forced down to the level of mediocrity? How can you ensure that the best become mentors to the rest?

▼ **Strategy:** To mark the opening of a new Harvey Nichols store, the stop-motion stars of the Wallace & Gromit movies posed for these web ads.

Client Harvey Nichols | Agency DDB

Talking point: Imagine that tomorrow your team suddenly takes on stars in the footballing class of David Beckham or Cristiano Ronaldo. In what ways would they help to raise motivation, teamwork and quality to their own level? What could your team learn from watching the best football teams in the world?

ACCESS TO THE GLOBAL BRAIN

Knowledge brokers act as a sort of interface between the problem and the solution. They acquire facts which can inspire the team with new impetus and information, and these in turn may open up new sources of ideas that your competitors do not have access to.

A knowledge broker or infomediary is an invaluable partner for any creative team. Alongside traditional media, brokers predominantly use the internet as an inexhaustible source of information: they will do their research in databases, virtual museums, sound and video libraries, forums, patent registry offices, international laboratories, online galleries, film archives, and any other source of knowledge they can find. They are experienced 'librarians' who can create order out of the almost infinite chaos of information, recognize what is valuable, and put together everything that is likely to be useful. If, for instance, you're planning an original design for a sports shop, a knowledge broker might focus on researching new lighting technology, materials, sound installations, even smells. They can also provide the team with the latest information on social trends, design and visual communications, and often seem to have a sixth sense, knowing just how to get the data that's required on any topic that's under consideration. But the knowledge broker's main task is to process all this information in such a way that it will act as a spur to the creatives. This means setting up a kind of creative laboratory to brew up the formula for inspiration. Knowledge-brokering is not a part-time task that someone can do on the side. It needs to be viewed as a profession in itself, requiring specific talents. The knowledge broker should become an integral member of the team, providing a connection between your agency and the facts, feelings and moods of the global brain.

◀ **Strategy:** Lichtfaktor is an artists' collective that works with light sources of various kinds: LEDs, flashlights, cycle lamps and Xenon lights. Using long exposure times, they create impressive photographic images with lightwriting or light drawing. Films can also be made using a similar technique.

Talking point: If you jump on a bandwagon today, the chances are that you're already too late and you'll join the also-rans. A knowledge broker can root out new technologies, materials, and social trends before other people have latched on to them.

Credits Alberto Meda & Francisco Gómez Paz

▶ **Strategy:** This innovative bottle uses the power of the sun's ultraviolet rays to disinfect polluted drinking water.

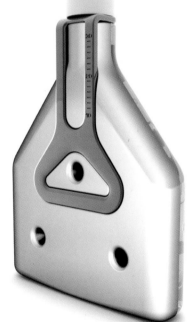

Talking point: Creatives in a meeting will generally call on their own experiences. However these all rely on knowledge gained in the past. Every day there are dozens of new inventions, materials and technologies emerging, but creative teams are often unaware of most of them.

MIX UP YOUR TEAM INTO NEW COMBINATIONS

Is it in the nature of creatives to work like drones on the same everyday tasks, thinking about the same everyday subjects? Then why is this the routine of most creative teams?

In the creative departments of most large agencies you will find creatives working on projects for particular clients in fixed units. Often they have been doing the same thing with the same people for years on end. Experience has shown, however, that it can be highly beneficial if sometimes the members of one team work with those of another. Turn your creatives into nomads, so that they don't settle into a comfort zone but are constantly coming together and communicating in different combinations. The consequences can be amazing: routine is replaced by fun, and meetings are suddenly flooded with fresh ideas. It also creates a palpable drop in tension for newcomers: their new workmates are not clients who need to be impressed and so they themselves will not feel solely responsible for the outcome of a project. Some directors will argue that every team is already perfectly adjusted to the needs of particular clients, and so it would be a backward step to have to initiate new members into the existing scheme of things. This might be true for account handling and in the final implementation phase, but it certainly isn't true for idea development.

Client **IKEA** | Agency Jung von Matt

▲ **Strategy:** The living room shown on the cover of the IKEA catalogue was replicated in three dimensions and taken on tour through 24 towns in Germany. Passers-by could have their photos taken on the set and were later sent a personalized copy of the catalogue with themselves as cover stars.

Talking point: What simple rules could be put into place to let your colleagues know that they will be moved from team to team in order to keep things fresh and give a new slant to old ideas?

Client **LEGO Systems** | Agency Blackdot

▲ **Strategy:** In this children's book, some well-loved fairytales were printed in special fluorescent ink that was only visible in the dark. This made the book an ideal companion for kids who like to read under the bedclothes.

Talking point: Set up lightning meetings with just two or three people standing in the kitchen, corridor or canteen. Basic rule: with complex projects, or if you're working for a longstanding client, it can make sense for just a single member of the team to be given all the details.

◀ **Strategy:** The Lego Power Miners online game takes children into an underground world where they can dig for crystals or fight against stone monsters. The game is a companion piece to the Power Miners construction set, and shows children what sort of adventures they can create for themselves.

Talking point: If you ask three teams of two people to put together their separate thoughts about this online game, you will get three totally different approaches. Make use of the fact that no two teams will think alike, and keep changing the partnerships in order to generate new ideas.

Teamwork gives you wings. If people have fun sparking ideas off one another, they will explore new realms of creative innovation. If you've never seen a team working this way, you must be missing a vital ingredient – trust!

A number of surveys have concluded that teams in creative meetings often come up with fewer ideas than when individuals scour their imaginations in isolation. Having worked with hundreds of teams, I can say from experience that this is only partly true, and there is a simple way to reverse this trend: if you can create an atmosphere of trust in your team, you will be able to lure them into being politically incorrect, breaking rules, overstepping boundaries, and basically doing everything they would never normally dare to do in everyday life. This process often begins with the thought of what fun it would be to cross lines and do things you're not supposed to do. This may make some team members nervous, and so the concept will only work if everyone has confidence in everyone else and your group has been able to form a kind of secret society. I have seen teams like this produce a host of great ideas which far exceed what any isolated individual might come up with. Here are a few suggestions for your 'secret society':

- There should never be more than four people at a creative meeting. If properly chaired, a team should produce so many ideas than any more participants would only stem the tide of inspiration.
- Creatives are often introverts, so a small group will encourage them to think and speak more freely. People are more confident in small groups.
- Avoid including executive directors in meetings of this kind, because their dominance and authority may well result in only one view being allowed.
- Work against any group tendency to 'fit in'. As the creative director, you need to set an example and take pleasure in breaking rules and encouraging a variety of viewpoints.
- If the members of your team still seem reluctant to go against the grain, try the following: during the search for ideas, ask them to think about how they might help solve the problem using their own bodily fluids. If that doesn't break the ice, perhaps they should look for another job.
- David versus Goliath. Forge your team into a secret society by banding together against the threat of a common enemy: market leaders, competitors, and any other baddies you can think of.

- Strategy: 'Dry Clean Only.'

Client *CITY* Magazine | Photographer **Ted Sabarese**

Talking point: Would you walk through a crowded shopping mall in a costume like this? No, neither would I. But of course it's an entirely different situation if there's a carnival on and the whole town is parading through the streets. At a meeting, presenting a completely crazy idea requires almost as much courage as going out in fancy dress when everyone else is in normal clothes. Only an atmosphere of complete trust and shared principles will give your team members the confidence to come up with suggestions that break all the rules.

◀ **Strategy:** 'Not So
Sweet. Toblerone Dark.'

**NOT SO
SWEET**
TOBLERONE
TOBLERONE DARK.

Talking point: Would your team embrace an idea like
this? Or are they so geared to convention that they
would categorically reject taboo themes?

▶ **Strategy:** Print ad
for Weber hats.

It's the hat.

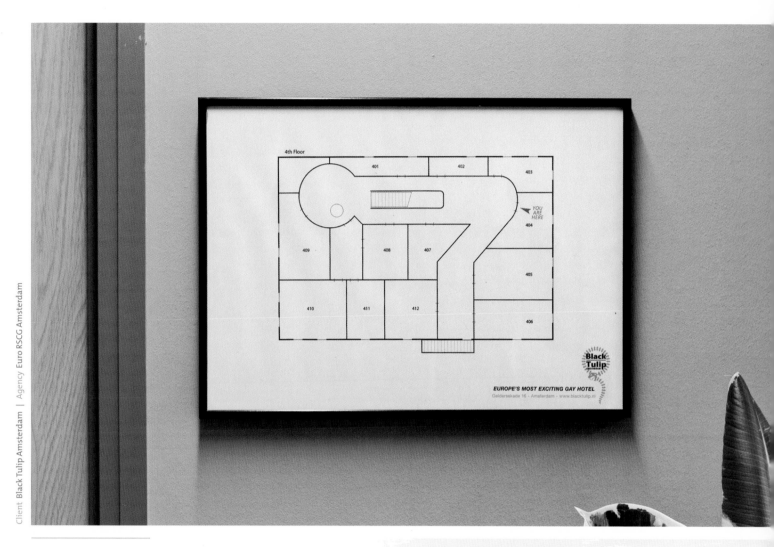

Client Black Tulip Amsterdam | Agency Euro RSCG Amsterdam

▲ Strategy: 'Black Tulip
Amsterdam. Europe's
Most Exciting Gay Hotel.'

Talking point: In any group, it's the majority that
decides what 'normal' is. If you want to cross particular
boundaries, it's the team leader who must insist on
looking beyond everyday standards.

IT DOESN'T FEEL LIKE WORK IF YOU'RE HAVING FUN

It's hard to imagine wonderful and witty ideas springing from a room full of grim-faced people. But your team are there to work, not to enjoy themselves – aren't they?

Humour makes people relax, and laughter makes anything bearable. Everyone should know the feeling you get when high spirits become so contagious that every word seems like a running gag. People have tears in their eyes, and the task in hand becomes a bit of fun instead of a tedious chore. The reward for this labour of love is a relaxed atmosphere and people sparking ideas off each other. Stale teams deliver stale ideas, and we consumers (because all of us are consumers) get sick and tired of the same old ads that agencies shove down our throats day after day. Creative meetings should never be routine. Routine begets routine. Every meeting should be exciting – a little emotion helps to shake things up and get people seeing themselves and their work in a different light. Humour is certainly one of the most positive ways of stimulating your team. Strangely, however, outsiders don't like seeing people laughing during meetings, because they think it means that you're not working, or not taking your work seriously. Ridiculous, but true. You're supposed to look deadly earnest and stressed out if you want to impress those who don't know what creativity is all about. And yet there are plenty of reasons why humour pays off: it gets rid of tension and aggression, and opens up new points of view. If it's fun, it's not work, complain many bosses. If it's fun, it's not work, agree many creatives, thereby giving their job a brand new dimension.

Client Arge Pilot | Agency Grey

◀ **Strategy:** Water-resistant pen from Pilot.

Talking point: It's sometimes a good idea to reverse the principle of cause and effect. Teams normally devote themselves intensively to coming up with something original, and only when they've succeeded do they sit back and relax. In other words, ideas are the cause, and relaxation is the effect. If you do things the other way round, you might be surprised at the results. Start off with a relaxing laugh, and the ideas will come with a lot less time and effort.

▶ **Strategy:** Colgate decided to give away ice creams instead of product samples. When you've eaten the ice cream, you find yourself holding the toothbrush-shaped stick, which reminds you to clean your teeth.

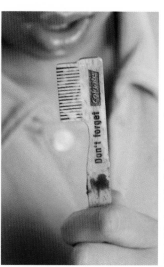

Client Colgate – Palmolive | Agency Y&R

Talking point: With many ad campaigns, websites and events, you often get the feeling that someone is desperately trying to force their products onto you. Do you think enjoyable ideas are more likely to emerge from a grim atmosphere or a light-hearted one?

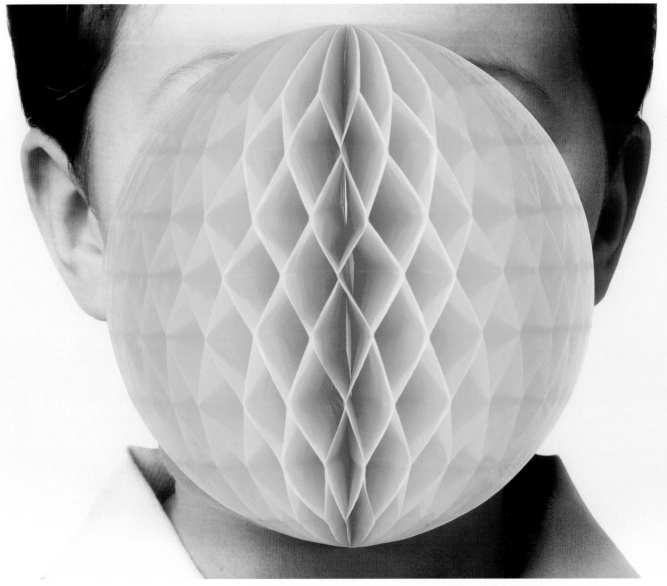

▲ **Strategy:** Double-page
ad for Big Big Bubble Gum.

Talking point: How can you organize meetings in the future to ensure
the sort of happy and relaxed atmosphere that will rub off on the ideas?

SOLVE PROBLEMS THAT DON'T EXIST YET

No time for fun and games – that's the equivalent of the plague in modern creative industries. And yet apparently pointless activities can be turned into priceless ideas.

Strengthen your team by regularly giving them what they dream of: complete creative freedom. Many agencies are full of talented people who feel like Ferraris being forced to drive through a 30-miles-an-hour zone. The frustration that builds up over the years should be obvious to everyone. All the more reason why from time to time you should turn the usual routine on its head. The results may be startling. Normally a client comes with a particular problem that requires a solution. Well, why not start off with a solution, and then look for a client with a suitable problem, or for a target group that might have been waiting for an idea like that to come along? In the advertising business, this principle is far from new: the thinking behind it is that ingenious concepts that have been implemented often carry off major awards at festivals. In any case there are plenty of good reasons why once or twice a month you should give your team a free rein:

▶ Working without the restrictions of a specific commission is a little like fitness training for creatives – it prevents the frustrations of routine tasks, and gives people pleasure and a renewed sense of motivation.

▶ If they're freed from rules and restrictions, your team can act as troubleshooters, helping other departments or partner firms to solve their own problems. Variety is the spice of life, after all.

▶ One suggestion: twice a month, your team could build up a pool of ideas for potential clients that you'd like to have on your books. You can take as many risks as you like, since you have nothing to lose but could have a great deal to gain.

▶ It can also be an interesting exercise to develop new projects for existing clients, even though they haven't asked for them yet and may have no plans along those lines. Your original idea could help them to open up new avenues.

▶ Do your team members have ideas for new products, campaigns or services arising out of their own personal interests? Once or twice a month, give them the chance to work freely on these ideas. They could be developed into something that your agency could use.

Credits Anton Alvarez, Yuko Maki, Robert Ek, Olle Gustafsson, Jaya Karlsson

▲ Strategy:
A McDonald's meal
made out of cardboard.

Talking point: Does your team still have the ability to work on crazy, impractical ideas like this one, or do your creatives shake their heads and walk away?

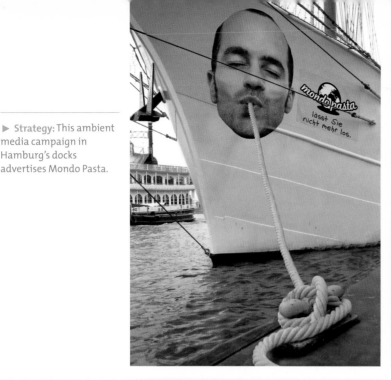

▶ **Strategy:** This ambient media campaign in Hamburg's docks advertises Mondo Pasta.

Talking point: Set up an internal database of ideas that no one has ever used, asked for, or will consciously go looking for. Stock it with rejected ideas from the past and brand-new flights of fancy, and eventually it will turn into a treasure chest that people can dip into when they're looking for answers to specific questions.

◀ **Strategy:** Luminex developed a light-emitting fabric that can be used for coats, shirts, bags, curtains and even tablecloths.

Talking point: Creatives can get a lot of fun from developing ideas for other professional fields or unusual projects. What new ideas might they come up with, using a material like Luminex? Could they find a practical application for it within your own field?

TRY TO UNDERSTAND HOW CREATIVITY WORKS

A fish in a pond doesn't feel trapped because it doesn't know anything about the world beyond the edges of the pond. If you want to swap your apparent freedom for true freedom, start by exploring the edges of your own personal pond.

Hundreds of books, seminars, lectures and TV documentaries deal with the subject of creativity, but very few creatives ever bother to find out what scientists, psychologists, their fellow professionals, artists or researchers have to say about it. This is strange if you bear in mind that creativity is the most important tool of their trade. Are designers, advertising directors, marketing managers and TV producers afraid that something bad might happen if they start analysing the creative process? Would it mean the end of their myth and their mystique? If I had to choose between two job applicants, I would go for the one who knows how to structure the creative process. Even if the other applicant seemed at first sight to have the more impressive portfolio, nevertheless my vote would go to the one who knew the source of his or her inspiration, how it could be given the right shape, how creative methods work, and how creative people can best stimulate one another. The less creatives know about these matters, the greater the risk that they will get stuck within their own invisible boundaries and keep swimming around in the same old circles.

How people often describe their own creativity: 'I prefer complete freedom to work, because that's the only way I can fulfil my creative potential to its fullest extent. Creativity isn't something you can actually grasp or control, and I don't have any particular method for developing ideas.'

What I hear when people describe creativity like this: 'I don't understand the hidden framework of rules, values and standards that I usually work within when developing ideas. Because I can't see those boundaries, I often mistakenly believe that I have unlimited creative freedom and can do absolutely anything.'

▼ Strategy: To sell ad spots for the film *Around the World in 80 Days*, a TV channel sent direct mails that travelled around the world before they reached the media planners they were addressed to.

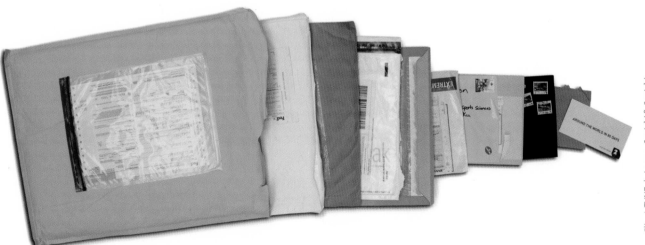

Client **TVNZ** | Agency Saatchi & Saatchi

Talking point: Understanding what goes on inside you when you develop ideas is a way of getting to know your own limitations. The rules and principles that govern your creative methods are at least as significant as your need for freedom.

▲ **Strategy:** This ad metaphorically shows that Amway Persona toothbrushes can solve the problem of food stuck in the gaps between your teeth.

Talking point: Look at these two ads, and decide what the dominant factor that inspired their originators could have been. Was it simply unlimited creative freedom, or was it a set of experiences, cultural rules and internal standards that they might not even have been aware of?

▲ Strategy:
Heinz Hot Ketchup.

Client Heinz | Agency Leo Burnett

SET UP A SPECIAL CREATIVE TASKFORCE

What would happen to your agency if you set up a flexible team with an unusual degree of freedom, lots of creative energy, and a quick grasp of all the essentials? Maybe a team like that could turn many a crisis situation into a great solution.

In the immortal words of Robert Burns, '*The best laid schemes o' mice an' men / Gang aft a-gley.*' Two days before a presentation, people start to have doubts about the main idea behind a campaign, or a new project seems to exceed the skills of your team, or the client has a sudden crisis and absolutely has to have the perfect solution within a matter of hours instead of days. Your team members are already working at full throttle, and there's no way they can take on another job, or they've bled themselves dry over another project – so what do you do? You send for your Special Creative Taskforce. Fresh, efficient, and raring to go, they can tackle any endangered project. This special unit is made up of people from different departments and teams, and can come together at a moment's notice, whenever a project is at risk. The brightest sparks are used to deadlines, have practised this sort of mission over and over again, and know exactly what steps must be taken when. As soon as the job is done, they will disband as quickly as they came together, and will return to their usual posts. Special Taskforces are particularly important for large agencies who have enough staff to create a talent pool. In smaller agencies, the force can be made up of top-class freelancers recruited from different fields. But one thing is clear – only the best will do.

▲ **Strategy:** The Coke Zero
Game looks just like a TV
ad, and uses individual
video sequences to take
the player through the
different levels.

Client Coca-Cola Germany | Agency North Kingdom

Talking point: What arguments are there against using a Special Taskforce
to support teams who have run out of steam or are faced with impossible
deadlines? If you're afraid that your exhausted team will come up with
something substandard, bring in the Taskforce to inject a little fire!

Client **Hatari Electric** | Agency **Lowe**

Talking point: The simplest and most obvious solutions often escape teams who have been working too long and too hard on the same subject. The aim of the Special Taskforce is to give them a creative shot in the arm.

Client **It's My Party** | Agency **GJP Advertising + Design**

CREATIVE CELLS WITH A FIXED SHELF LIFE

What do a fashion show by Karl Lagerfeld, a film by Guy Ritchie, and a building by Zaha Hadid have in common? Ambitious leaders gather a dream team around themselves in order to implement a brilliant piece of work. Afterwards, they all go their separate ways.

Short-term teams are most famously found in the film industry, where each director assembles an ideal cast and crew that lasts only as long as the production. The lengthy process of casting and appointing the production team takes place at the beginning, and this is what determines the course, quality and ultimate success of the film. In many branches of the creative industries, however, this is not how things are done. Generally teams or partnerships are fixed, have been together for long periods, and have worked for particular clients on specific projects. The advantage of flexible teams like those found in fashion, theatre or film is obvious: for each project you assemble the best possible people for the job, and the very tran-

sience of the group can create strong motivation and team spirit. If the structure of your agency doesn't allow for this kind of cooperation, it might be worth considering whether at least three or four times a year it could be worth your while to take the best people out of your established teams and use them on specially selected projects that will enhance their own prestige. Those who are allowed to take part will get respect, variety, a sense of privilege and motivation, and above all a lot of fun out of the experience. When the project is finished, the team will be disbanded and the members will return to their original groups. When the next suitable project comes up, you can repeat the process with a new crew.

IMMER OFFEN FÜR NEUES.

DAS NEUE MINI CABRIO. IMMER OFFEN.

Die Weltpremiere des neuen MINI Cabrio findet dieses Mal an einem ganz besonderen Ort statt: direkt in Ihren Händen! Halten Sie diese Anzeige unter www.MINI.de/webcam vor Ihre Webcam und schon erleben Sie das neue MINI Cabrio aus sämtlichen Perspektiven – live und in 3D. Sie glauben das nicht? Probieren Sie es aus!

◄ **Strategy:** This interactive print campaign for Mini Cabrio. uses augmented reality technology to build a bridge between the real and digital worlds, so that a three-dimensional product can be seen on a two-dimensional ad. When viewed by the online webcam, the Mini Cabrio appears as a virtual model, and lets you turn it over in your hands to see all the details.

Talking point: To give new impetus to your creative meetings, form two teams of volunteers and get them to compete against each other. The final results can be assessed according to criteria that have been laid down beforehand.

◄ **Strategy:** The Fiat 500 'Interactive Poster' invites passers-by to send a text message: 'I'm a Turiner. Text me, Berliner.' The message can then be seen by the public as it moves across an LCD ticker.

Talking point: If you're looking for unusual ideas like this, you could hold occasional 'auditions' for freelancers, to ensure you get the best possible person for a particular project. Freelancers can boost your team for the duration of the project.

▶ **Strategy:** A new Toyota was launched with a 3D installation on the side of a high-rise block. The display was accompanied by music and a spectacular aerial dance show.

THE LAW OF TWO FEET

Creatives are unusual people: early in the morning they're positively bursting with ideas, but as soon as they walk into their first meeting, all their ideas dry up.

Open Space Technology (OST) is a highly effective method of structuring discussions and conferences, developed by Harrison Owen. I would like to borrow one marvellously simple rule from OST which ought to become integral to every creative team: the Law of Two Feet. It means that if you're in a meeting but not learning nor contributing anything, you are free to use your feet and walk out at any time without needing an excuse. There's no point in staying unless it seems worthwhile or productive to do so. If this step seems too drastic, just think how many hours you have already wasted just because some annoying person was blocking your every move and couldn't or wouldn't see sense. But if you reserve the right to get up and go, you'll be able to use your time more use-fully elsewhere, and the meeting may also get an energy boost because the only people left will be those who are actively engaged. Harrison Owen tells the following story about the origin of Open Space: he had just successfully chaired a conference for 200 event organizers when one participant gave him a crucial piece of feedback: the conference went well, but the best part of it was the coffee breaks. Owen couldn't get this remark out of his head, and so he began to think about how to organize a conference consisting of nothing but coffee breaks. This format should become a basic element of creative meetings, both to increase productivity and to create an atmos-phere which will automatically be more relaxed and enjoyable for all involved.

▶ Strategy: The Xbox game *Gears of War 2* was promoted with specially designed shipping containers placed at various sites, attracting new players and allowing them to immerse themselves in a parallel world.

Client Microsoft | Agency Kumar Manix, Rinsed Studio

Talking point: Allow your colleagues to walk out of unproductive meetings before they walk out on you and the agency. Give plenty of advance notice for meetings on exciting projects or interesting clients, and open them up to all your colleagues. Those who express an interest beforehand should be in on the idea development phase. Making participation voluntary increases motivation and acceptance of responsibility, and thus also increases the potential quality of the work.

PUTTING A TEAM TOGETHER: A MATTER OF CHEMISTRY

You can't tie a knot with one hand, according to an ancient Mongolian proverb. Even with two hands, it can sometimes be a complicated business. However, with six, eight or twelve hands, it would be almost impossible.

Teams are complex. Their make-up and their environment will determine how they develop and grow. Some are wellsprings of new ideas, while others make you feel hemmed in and desperate to escape. Clearly the chemistry of the group is a big factor, but how this actually works is often a mystery. There are, however, a few basic rules that govern team chemistry, and the following questions should help you pin them down:

▶ Imagine that you're a team leader from a rival agency. What would you do to ensure that the people attending a meeting don't listen to one another? Make a list of the most common forms of sabotage, and then look for ways of improving the atmosphere at your own meetings.

▶ Try looking into the future, and imagine that a shared vision and enthusiasm has forged your col-leagues into a dream team. What is their attitude towards one another, and how can you tell that they share a vision?

▶ If people are unsure about their roles in the team, what would you need to do to make them feel even more insecure and totally confused about where they stand?

▶ Do you know why your team often makes such slow progress at meetings? Try to work out all the unwritten rules, and write them down somewhere that everyone can see them.

▶ Is your team generally able to resolve conflicts without any help from outside? If not, what stops them? Exactly what needs to be changed in order to ensure that they develop this ability?

▶ Does your team have any idea of its status within the agency? What concrete signs can it be given, and in what form does the agency present its feedback to your team members?

▶ How would an outsider know that the personal goals of some of your colleagues do not coincide with those of the team at large? What would be the quickest way to bring them back into line?

▶ Do members of your team ever hide their true intentions during discussions? What would have to be done if you wanted to make everyone suspicious of everyone else, and make communication totally impossible?

▶ If other departments don't have a clue what your team actually does and under what conditions it works best, what effect does that have on your team and its work?

▶ Imagine that from now on, all your creative meetings will be well structured. What would have to

change in the agency, and who has most to gain from this change?

▶ What impact would it have on projects, teams and the agency if every individual team member was in exactly the right position to use their talents to maximum effect?

▶ If your team members failed to recognize or respect your leadership, what would be the consequences for the project and for team cooperation as a whole?

▶ What effect would it have if your team members offered you totally honest feedback concerning your qualities as a director? What kind of feedback would be most productive?

▶ How would an outsider recognize that your team is able to relax and balance its priorities? How could you help your team to get this balance right?

Get them off
your dog.

FRONTLINE
FLEA & TICK SPRAY
available at JAKPETZ

RM9.90

CREATIVE BRIEFING

04

There are three kinds of account handler. Some bombard the client right from the start with their all-knowing answers. Others try to ask a few questions. But only account handlers who know which questions are worth asking can come up with the answers that will lead to great solutions.

There are many different views and expectations concerning the duties of an account handler on the one hand, and the rights and responsibilities of the client on the other. However, as I see it, when a project gets underway, the roles are pretty clear: the account handler should steer the conversation with relevant questions, listen carefully to the answers, maintain interest and enthusiasm, and gradually guide the client's thoughts into some kind of order. Apart from the questions, the client should do most of the talking, because the client is the only person who fully understands the problem that led to your agency being hired in the first place. If you start off giving answers rather than asking relevant questions, you won't fully understand the underlying problems or exactly what you are supposed to do about them, and consequently you won't be able to come up with a practical strategy or a clear target for your creative team. It's a process that requires a real talent for coaching, questioning techniques and counselling.

It always amazes me that some account handlers still go into meetings expecting clients to know every aspect of their field, their products, the market, the competition, and advertising in general. In reality, the very first conversation will often leave the account handler in a state of shock: clients often have no clear idea of what they actually want, let alone of the way to achieve it. They can't pinpoint the true heart of the problem, or can't grasp it in its entirety. Often they aren't even sure of their own role in this introductory meeting, and bombard the account handler with vast quantities of irrelevant information. They might bring a brief that contains everything and nothing, or which is so vague that it would still apply if it were under the logo of any of their competitors. But never forget, it's the clients' right to be like this, because the customer is never wrong! The art of the account handler is to guide clients, to help them structure information, to reduce the complexity of the project, to tease out all the missing facts and bring clarity to confusion. By the end, there should be two items on the table: firstly, a clear goal and strategy that the clients are happy with and the team can work with; secondly, all the underlying issues should have been brought to light, so that there will be no unforeseen hitches later on.

A lot of account handlers still seem to think their job consists of offering clients the benefit of their knowledge and experience, explaining how they've solved similar problems in the past, and recommending their own preferred course of action. It can only be hoped that this approach will soon become a thing of the past. If taken, this kind of advice only leads to the agency repeating the same old procedures, with no regard for originality or the intended goal. It's also easy to overlook the client's real needs, because any underlying problems may be glossed over instead of brought to light. Finally and most importantly, if clients themselves are not willing to take advice or to examine the problems in detail, even the most professional of account handlers has no hope of success.

◀ Strategy: This display makes use of kitchen utensils to illustrate the point that IKEA are cutting, peeling and shredding their prices.

Talking point: What questions should an account handler ask to open up new avenues for clients that they would not have been willing to explore before?

Lend a hand,
let them hold
on to life!

Lend a hand,
let them hold
on to life!

◄ **Strategy:** 'Lend a hand, let them hold on to life!' is the strapline of this direct marketing campaign for a children's aid charity.

Client **KMCV** | Agency *Magma Istanbul*

EVOLUTION OR REVOLUTION?

According to the psychologist Abraham Maslow, if all you have is a hammer, everything looks like a nail. This may explain why many agencies feel that every brief is actually a creative challenge to come up with a masterpiece.

Dear clients, please do not ask for creativity and then turn your noses up at it. However, perhaps in future we should use the term with a little more discrimination. It should be made clear right from the start what kind of creativity the client is after, bearing in mind that conscientious designers, photographers and directors see every task as a new creative challenge. Clients often fan the creative flames by announcing in all seriousness that they want something totally revolutionary, whereas in fact all they want is a small alteration to the status quo. To them, moving the chairs around amounts to a revolution. This view of creativity inevitably leads to false expectations, and hence to a series of presentations involving repeated failures and a great deal of frustration for the creatives themselves. Whether you represent the client or the agency, make sure that future projects are clearly labelled, and the degree of originality required is agreed before the work begins. From the countless briefings and discussions I myself have taken part in, I can divide creative contracts into three basic forms:

- ▶ Search and select
- ▶ Evolution: variations and modifications
- ▶ Revolution: radical innovations

You and your client should decide whether the project simply involves searching for or selecting from existing ideas. For instance, if a soft drinks bottle needs a new colour, is this a question of finding new ideas or simply choosing which colour would be right? Evolution entails modifying or developing an existing model: for instance, working out a different shape for a stand at a trade fair, or for a display case. Revolution means a radical break with the past: for example, a client may be planning a totally new way of displaying products in a public space, incorporating the residential and office buildings in the city centre.

Things that clients say:
'We want great ideas – preferably ones
that have already been successful.'

What creatives hear:
'We want great ideas – preferably ones
that no one's ever seen before.'

Client illy | Creative Adam Kalkin

◀ **Strategy:** The illy Push Button House is a completely functional home that has been built inside a standard cargo container. At the push of a button, the container unfolds to its full extent in just 90 seconds.

Talking point: As there are no internationally recognized standards for what constitutes creativity, it can sometimes be useful to ask the following question: On a scale of 0 to 10, with 10 standing for radical creativity (such as the Illy house) and 0 for minimal change, what rating would you give your project?

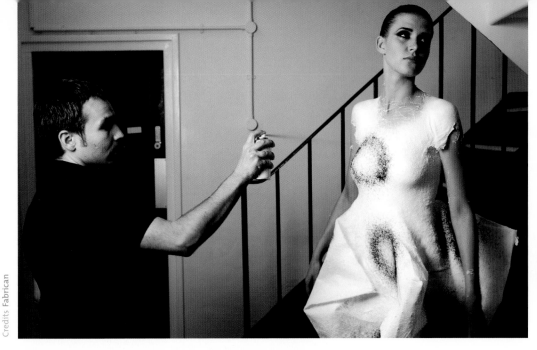

Credits Fabrican

Talking point: If you can establish the degree of creativity that the client requires right from the start, you may save your team a great deal of time, money and nervous energy.

◀ **Strategy:** Spray-on fabric in a can! Manuel Torres invented a liquid that can be sprayed on to the body and instantly forms thousands of fibres that combine to create a fabric. This can then be detached from the body as a ready-made garment that fits like a second skin.

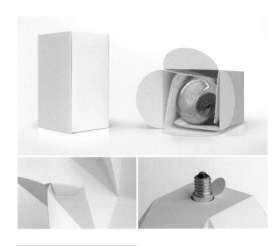

▲ **Strategy:**
The packaging for this light bulb can also be used as a lampshade.

Client Muji | Agency SiebertHead Ltd

Talking point: Ask three different people (a client, a colleague, a friend) to give this packaging a mark out of 10 for creativity. You will probably get three different answers, which only goes to show how important it is to agree on a level at the start of each project.

When your clients come to a meeting and tell you with a radiant smile that they want to start a spectacular online community, just ask one simple question: why?

Let's imagine that your client is a network operator in the IT industry, and he springs it on you that he wants to start an online community to provide a long-term link-up with the top 20 per cent of his customers. At the first briefing he informs you that he's already got the whole thing planned, and all he needs is a concrete design for what the site should actually look like. This may be your first and last chance to ask the magic question: why an online community? If truth be told, this is actually the client's first attempt to solve a problem which has lain dormant below the surface until now. But here's the dilemma: you can only find the right way to solve a problem if you can see every part of it. At the start, nobody actually knows whether an online community is the right answer. Which brings us to the next question. Why has it suddenly become necessary to create a long-term link-up with regular customers? The client might respond that he's beginning to lose out to the competition. So why are regular customers suddenly going over to the opposition? Well, four weeks ago they all received a very

appealing offer. What was so special about this offer that it seduced all these good customers? It introduced a new loyalty programme for people who make a lot of phone calls. So what difference does this system make to all the good customers? If they switch over, they'll get a much better deal. And there we have the problem in a nutshell: all those loyal customers are going over to the other side because they're being offered a very attractive loyalty programme. So far so good. Then what is the client's real aim? He will reply: to stop our customers from leaving us. And what's the solution he's brought with him to the meeting? That's right, an online community. And this brings us back to our first question: why? Is an online community, with a few nice gifts and free games, really the best way to get customers to stay loyal? Don't make me laugh! But at least now that we've grasped the basic problem, we can start asking the right questions that will lead us to the right solution. From this example, you can see what might happen if a client brings a pet solution to the briefing without first having fully analysed the original problem and all its roots. If the agency doesn't realize this, chances are that they will go ahead with the campaign or project as requested by the client, and the end result will be failure. So Rule Number One for the first meeting is: if clients bring their own solutions, insist on examining the underlying problem down to the very last detail. Only then will you be able to judge whether their solution is the best one or not. If it isn't, use the knowledge you've gained to find new and different approaches and work with them.

▲ Strategy: 'Treatment to care for your hands.' This direct mail shows that the best way to look after your hands is to use Spontex rubber gloves.

Client Spontex | Agency Reskala y Asociados

Talking point: A great idea, but what problem does it set out to solve? Is direct marketing the best way to solve that problem, or are there other more effective ways in which this could be done?

Fix your broken

BRIGHTON
language school

www.braiton.ru

▲ **Strategy:** 'Fix your broken English. Polish your rusty Deutsch. Brighton Language School.'

Polish your rusty

BRIGHTON
language school

www.braiton.ru

Client Brighton Language School | Agency Voskhod

Talking point: An effective client consultation carries with it the risk that what was intended as a print campaign may end up turning into a direct mail or online campaign, thus wasting the resources already spent on it. That is why many account handlers prefer to go along with the clients' wishes, if they know from the start that a print campaign is what they want. What are your own account handler's priorities: the best solution, or a deal with the client?

A QUESTION OF PROFESSIONALISM

'I'm positive that the best way to drive brand engagement is to go viral with this, but I'm not feeling the cross-media commitment that will really push our brand values. And the messaging architecture isn't transparent enough.'

A marketing director

If I'd been at that meeting, I wouldn't have understood a word. And I'd like to invite anyone who claims that they did to take part in a little experiment: ask three of your colleagues to write down the meaning of the following terms: 'cross-media commitment', 'brand engagement', 'brand values', 'messaging architecture'. Then see if they all come up with the same definitions. Do they all agree, for instance, on what 'messaging architecture' consists of and how it functions? Even if they may all have similar ideas about 'brand values', you'll be amazed how differently they will interpret terms like reliability, originality, or market leadership. And what does 'going viral' actually mean? Are we sure we're all talking about the same thing? I reckon I can tell you the result of the test even before you hold it. Three different people will give you three different sets of answers. But even more important is the fact that at a meeting they will all use those buzzwords in their own fashion, and apply them to the project in hand in the same way.

This is where the issue of professionalism arises. None of the people at that meeting would have the nerve to ask exactly what these terms mean. Instead they would all nod knowingly as the terms are dropped, even though they haven't a clue what the speaker is talking about. A misconceived professionalism can lay the foundations for misunderstandings and eventual disasters. Account handlers are particularly prone to fall into this trap, because they are often anxious to impress the client with their knowledge and experience. In actual fact, account handlers are only competent and professional when they draw the client's attention to this trap and then proceed to ask the relevant questions.

The first step that account handlers need to take is to establish an atmosphere that will allow them to make a virtue out of their curiosity and lack of knowledge. Prepare clients beforehand by telling them to proceed as if you didn't know the first thing about the subject. Warn them that you are going to ask them questions that might sound naive and childish. This will give you the freedom to ask whatever you like, and so to get to the very bottom of the problems you are to deal with. You are starting out on a mission, and this means getting to know all the technical details. Questions are the tools of curiosity. Albert Einstein once said: 'I have no special talents. I am only passionately curious.' Every day, we all see light, but how many of us are curious and adventurous enough to ask what light actually is? Do you know? And yet it's such a simple question. Einstein tried to answer it, and in 1905 he discovered 'light quanta' or photons, a piece of work that later won him the Nobel Prize. You don't have to go that far, but if you ask the right questions at a briefing, it won't take long for you to root out problems and weak points, gain new perspectives, show everyone where the gaps are, and latch onto the basic priorities. One essential step here is to keep your vocabulary simple. When you're talking to clients, avoid empty buzzwords, abstract terms, foreign words and technical jargon. For me one of the give-away signs of incompetence is how much of jargon people inject into their conversation. True professionalism lies in presenting and explaining the most complex specialist subjects in such a way that even a layperson can understand what you're talking about perfectly.

Client Mercedes-Benz | Agency BBDO

The first brake that reads the street.

BAS PLUS – the new brake assist system with foresighted radar technology. As standard in the Mercedes-Benz S-Class.

Mercedes-Benz

◄ Strategy: This print campaign shows you at a glance what the BAS PLUS braking system does for Mercedes-Benz drivers.

Talking point: Try imagining all the technical terms that might have been used in the brief for this campaign, and ask yourself what they would have contributed to the clarity, originality and simplicity of this ad.

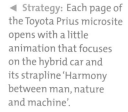

◀ **Strategy:** Each page of the Toyota Prius microsite opens with a little animation that focuses on the hybrid car and its strapline 'Harmony between man, nature and machine'.

Client **Toyota** | Agency **EVB/Saatchi & Saatchi**

Talking point: Imagine that every technical term used in your briefs and meetings was replaced by everyday words, and that these described your project so clearly that even the target group would have fun working on it.

Client **NBC Universal Global Networks** | Agency **Jung von Matt**

▲ **Strategy:** An installation inside the toilets at a nightclub: just before you go inside, the lights go out, plunging the room into darkness. Then you realize that you're standing right in the middle of a bloody crime scene. The message on the mirror reads: 'See what others don't see. 13th Street. The action and suspense channel.'

Talking point: Simplify your language. This is even more crucial now that the different branches of the creative industries are becoming increasingly interdependent. What communication skills would have helped the team that developed this ambient media campaign to take part in meetings involving new media, events, computer animation and trade fair architecture and yet still allowed them to work together without misunderstandings?

Written briefs are dead. Usually they only offer stereotypical answers to questions that nobody has ever asked.

With major projects especially, a written brief should be considered as little more than preparatory work to cover basic questions and key information. If you want to avoid digressions and time-consuming misunderstandings through the 'Chinese Whispers' effect, you and the client should organize a briefing workshop. This is the most direct method of getting to the point, and will help teams to produce the right kind of content in the shortest time. If properly run by client and creative director, it will also create an atmosphere in which the key questions can be openly discussed and the subject thoroughly explored. In my experience, a project such as a trade stand, a packaging design, an online campaign, a shop interior or an event is so complex that a written brief will simply leave most questions unanswered. The organizers of a workshop, on the other hand, can judge what information is required and thus save more time than they actually invest in the workshop itself. The clearer and more relevant the information that emerges from

these workshops, the fewer brief revisions and corrections will be necessary.

There is one more aspect to consider: I've seen very few briefs that truly fill creative teams with enthusiasm and inspiration, but workshops have a much better chance of getting them fired up and focused. By the end, not only should your team know their goal and have formulated a precise strategy to meet it, but they should also have a list of criteria which will enable them to identify which of their many ideas will hit the bull's eye during the evaluation phase. This list should be compiled right at the start and definitely not at the end. An interesting side effect of these workshops is that the clients also become heavily involved in briefing, strategy and targeting, meaning that they will be all the more committed to the final result. But a written brief alone is far too vague: you can say too much, you can say too little, and even the most detailed of outlines can end up lacking in colour and depth.

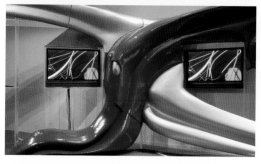

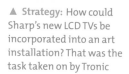

▲ **Strategy:** How could Sharp's new LCD TVs be incorporated into an art installation? That was the task taken on by Tronic Studio. The AQUOS™ Project was part of an international campaign, and was set up in a gallery in SoHo, New York.

Talking point: Written briefs can lead to using the same old techniques and worn-out jargon. How can you get people to take a new approach to briefs that will look forwards instead of backwards?

◀ Strategy: This print campaign shows at a glance how the new Golf 32 can power ahead.

Talking point: Many briefs are about as exciting as an instruction leaflet for prostate medication. How can you help the client add inspiration to information?

▼ Strategy: This 60-second viral by Tracfone shows someone putting a mobile phone into a microwave oven. Nothing happens for the first 20 seconds, and the tension mounts. Then the mobile melts, and the contents grow and mutate into a gruesome monster. As no brand is mentioned, many of the two million or so people who saw the video on YouTube had to go out of their way to find out the brand that was behind it.

Talking point: Written briefs tend to close doors rather than open them. This is especially so when the client and the agency have worked together for a long period of time. How could the client extend the field of play right from the start so that original ideas like this one might have a chance?

HOW ARE PROBLEMS DISCOVERED?

Just as a fish doesn't know that it's wet, we're not aware of most of the problems that surround us in our daily lives. The majority are such a familiar component of our everyday world that in some strange way, they become completely invisible.

Are you sitting comfortably? Before you assure me that you're nice and relaxed, make sure that it's really true. The fact is, it's often tiny things that escape our attention because of their sheer familiarity. If you delve into the details of even a simple question like 'Are you sitting comfortably?', you might well notice that there's something about your position that's actually uncomfortable, or even downright painful. So if my question has made you aware of a problem, congratulations! Now you can give some thought to finding an original solution to your seating problem.

It can sometimes be a very useful exercise to look for undiscovered problems, because generally we tend to act only when the trouble has already started and requires an urgent solution. This is why most of the time the creative industries are like a fire brigade, called on to tackle emergencies for their clients. It can

be a pleasant diversion simply to sit down with the client and look for pitfalls that nobody has noticed yet. This exercise might even lead to new designs or products that can overcome the difficulties. When have you ever taken the time to look for problems that lie hidden in shopping malls, children's toys, or computer games? The field is virtually boundless, because problems are everywhere. So just how do you set about discovering them? In my experience, the first requisite is a healthy dose of childlike curiosity. The young daughter of the American physicist Dr Edwin Herbert Land discovered an unsolved problem which gave rise to a revolutionary idea. She watched her father taking a photograph and asked if she could see it right away. Of course it wasn't possible then, but Land couldn't get her unfulfilled wish out of his mind. In 1947, he gave the world the first instant camera.

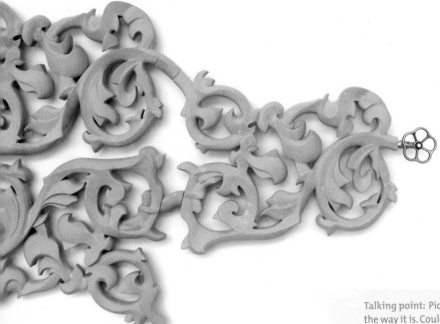

Credits Joris Laarman | Photo Rik Seisveld

◀ **Strategy:** A radiator that is also a striking decorative feature.

Talking point: Pick up any everyday object and ask yourself if it's perfect the way it is. Could it have a fault that most people simply ignore because they're so familiar with it?

Client **Prepara** | Agency **Pollen Design**

◀ **Strategy:** Nothing improves the taste of food more than fresh ingredients. The Prepara Herb-Savor prolongs the life of fresh herbs by up to three weeks.

Talking point: If you'd asked people in 1950 what improvements they'd like to see in their telephones, scarcely anyone would have thought of push-button dialling, an integrated answering machine, or mobile phones. This herb container is another great new idea. What obvious problems (or solutions) are there in your workplace that no one has noticed until now?

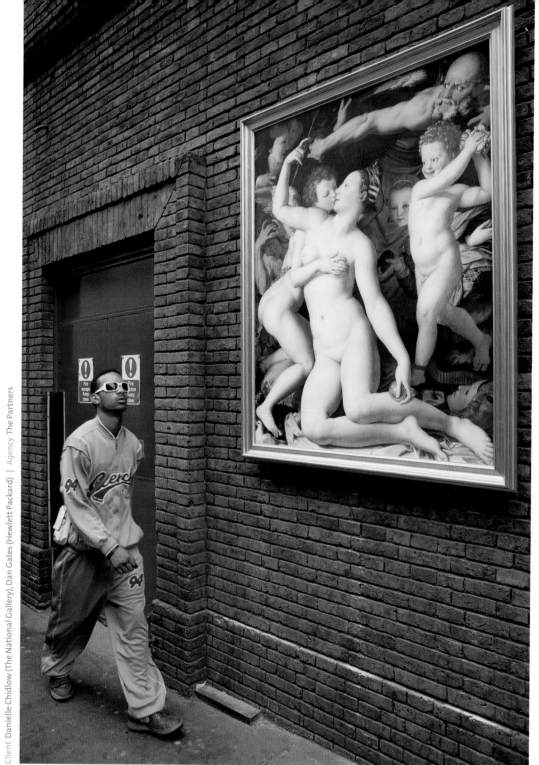

◀ Strategy: If people won't come to the museum, the museum must come to them. Reproductions of masterpieces from the National Gallery were put up at 44 different locations around London. A website offered downloadable tours, maps and audio commentaries on individual works.

Talking point: If you want to discover problems and understand them, learn to listen carefully to your target group. The cleverest solutions often arise spontaneously when you speak to these people and get to know exactly what they want.

YOU NEVER KNOW WHAT YOU DON'T KNOW

Imagine a fashion house commissions you to design a revolutionary new shopping concept that will create a sensation all over the world. Where would you choose to open the first store: Paris, New York, Tokyo or Dubai? Do you know what information you would need in order to make the right decision?

Sometimes, the participants in a creative briefing meeting get a feeling that ranges from indecision to total paralysis. They want a clear strategy or target, and may unfairly attribute the lack of these to the incompetence or even ill will of the people they're dealing with, but an experienced account handler will know that the confusion is usually due to a lack of information. It's hard to get a complete picture when pieces of the puzzle are missing. But if all the information is available, meaning that the situation can be examined from all sides, the decision will virtually make itself. If that doesn't happen, however, there is generally a great deal of insecurity, and it's essential that the account handler identifies this issue quickly, because whoever has to take the decision will often have recourse to a common device: namely, filling the gaps with assumptions and conjectures. Without timely intervention, these may swiftly be turned into facts, so your job is to make sure the guesses are replaced by certainties.

For instance, clients may say that most people who log onto their company website quit as soon as they see the homepage, because it contains an overload of information. Is this assertion a matter of knowledge or of speculation? If it's the latter, you really need to approach the target group directly, perhaps with a survey, to find out what they're really thinking. If you don't, you'll risk being led astray by the client's 'gut feelings', and so the project is doomed to failure from the start.

▲ **Strategy:** Creativity plays a major role in the computer game *LittleBigPlanet*: the strapline is 'Play, create, share'. Players are able to customize every detail of the game in the way they want and then share it with other players online.

Talking point: During a briefing meeting with clients, how can you tell whether the information they provide is a matter of fact or speculation? The more unproven assumptions find their way into the starting phase, the more likely they are to lead to errors and bad decisions. This applies particularly to complex projects like computer games, websites and store designs.

▶ **Strategy:** Villa Eugénie is an event-planning firm based in Belgium and internationally renowned for their extravagant and innovative fashion shows. Directed by Etienne Russo, this extraordinary fashion event took place before some 400 guests in the Istituto di Scienze Militari Aeronautiche, a building from the era of Mussolini. The 17-minute performance was partly inspired by the movie *Brazil*, and showcased 41 designs inspired by office life in 1950s Italy.

Talking point: I think...I believe...I presume...in my experience... These expressions crop up time and again during briefings, and for the most part they are a cover for unproven assumptions. If you were trying to come up with a new concept for a fashion show, ask yourself to what extent such assumptions might affect the project and its impact on the target group.

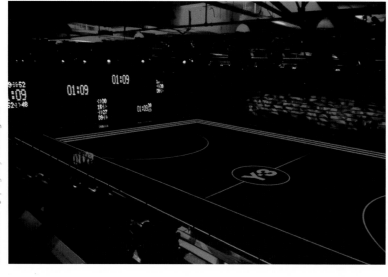

◀ **Strategy:** For the launch of Yohji Yamamoto's Adidas Y3 collection, event organizers Villa Eugénie decided to use the basketball court at Hunter College, New York. The playing area was transformed into a runway, and the audience was plunged into a fast-moving world of lights and motion.

FORMULATING A GOAL

If account handlers fail to formulate a goal in plain and simple terms, how can creatives be expected to develop an idea which will convey a plain and simple message to the target group within seconds?

Many teams start creative meetings along hopeful but rather disorganized lines: 'We don't know where we want to go, but that'll get us there quicker!' Vague, all-purpose goals are expected to produce miracles. The following three examples could be described as 'goals', but they are practically useless as far as a creative team is concerned:

▶ We need to improve our image.

▶ We want to sell more.

▶ We'd like to attract more customers.

These aspirations are far too abstract and general. They could apply to any company or brand. They supply no information at all, and they also throw up a large number of questions. A properly formulated goal reduces the complexities of the entire briefing process to one simple question, without any need for generalizations or technical terminology. It's only when you can reduce the goal to a simple sentence that you'll be able to develop a clear message that will quickly convince the target group. Here are four examples of well-formulated goals:

▶ What can we do to get trade-fair visitors over 50 years of age to play with our new games console?

▶ How can a website encourage children to recommend our low-calorie snack bar to their friends?

▶ How can we show in a print campaign that the new XR Supreme tyres offer the best road-holding in their class?

▶ How can we design the packaging for a medication to ensure that elderly people can see straight away whether its use-by date has expired?

Goals like these should be noted down and placed in a central position at creative meetings, so that everyone can see them. This increases clarity and keeps everyone's ideas moving in the same direction. Important information from the brief may also need to be reiterated verbally during meetings in order to avoid misunderstandings and perhaps spark off new ideas. Once the destination is known, the journey can begin at any point, and you can even follow a sidetrack that might lead you to new vistas or experiences. It's only people who don't know where they're going that have to stick to the beaten track for fear of getting lost. This is where creativity risks getting stuck in a rut, and the only practical course of action is to modify existing solutions. Here, then, are the seven most important rules for goal formulation, to give your team the best possible start:

▶ A well-formulated goal will always include a single-minded proposition.
▶ It will not contain any 'and'.
▶ It will always be in the form of a question.
▶ It should be phrased as succinctly as possible.
▶ It should be so simple that even a 12-year-old can understand it.
▶ If possible, it should not contain any foreign words or technical terms.
▶ It should stimulate creative ideas.

A single-minded proposition is essential because nowadays your target group will simply not have time for more information. Your campaign should focus on communicating just one aspect or benefit of the product. In these days of information overload, anything extra will either not be noticed or will detract from your main message. That is why there should be no 'and' in your goal. Whatever you come up with should be brief and to the point, and you should not stint on the time you invest in phrasing your goal. Woodrow Wilson put it very neatly: 'If I am to speak ten minutes, I need a week for preparation... if an hour, I am ready now.' It can be good practice to spend up to 30 per cent of the time available for a project on getting the right wording for your ultimate goal. It can often take you halfway to your ideal solution. But if the team or client is not sure how to do it, you could try two or three different formulations to generate different pools of ideas. The results will usually show you pretty soon if you are on the right track or not.

◄ **Strategy:**
STICK tea is a simple,
practical and hygienic
alternative to teabags.

Talking point: How would you design a modern and less cumbersome alternative to the teabag? If you don't think this goal is precise enough, see if you can phrase it differently. What would a teabag look like if you simply had to dip it in the cup and then take it out again? Polish this question until it is smooth and rounded and dazzling enough to inspire. Under no circumstances should you be satisfied with the first version you come up with.

► **Strategy:** For a
campaign entitled
'Bigger Storage Ideas',
the balconies of an
apartment block were
decorated to resemble
IKEA storage solutions.

Talking point: How could we show that IKEA offers lots of ideas to help you keep your home tidy? The first formulation often fails to convey the full goal, so it can make sense to work with more than one. Each formulation will open up a different perspective. Use two or three and work through them one by one until you are sure you have one that is best suited to the purpose.

Talking point: How can we show that Loctite's new superglue will stick things together more firmly than anything else? With a really great campaign, you should be able to grasp the goal within ten seconds without ever having seen the brief. Give yourself the time and opportunity to look at the best creative work at the Cannes Lions International Advertising Festival and guess how each goal was formulated.

▲ Strategy: Super Attak from Loctite, a glue that sticks in seconds.

▶ Strategy:
Legal Sea Foods.

Talking point: What do you think the goal was here? No prizes for guessing correctly, I'm afraid.

The East Greenwich Pendulum — Thursday, December 6, 2007 • Page 7-B

Astronomers find changes in Saturn's rings

Astronomers have discovered that Saturn's D ring, the innermost of Saturn's 15 rings, has grown dimmer in the past 25 years and sections have moved up to 125 miles inward toward the planet. This discovery was made after astronomers compiled results predominantly from the Voyager 2 spacecraft, which passed Saturn in 1981, and the Cassini-Huygens probe which entered Saturn's orbit last year. Other rings were found to be rotating slower than had previously been estimated with computer models. It was also discovered that the matter composing the rings is of far more widely varying temperatures than had been expected. Sections of Saturn's F ring were also recognised as breaking apart and reforming, depending on the location of one of Saturn's moons.

The rings, which are now iconic to Saturn, and known to be common to all Jovian planets in general, were first observed in 1610 by Galileo. The rings have recently become a subject of scientific interest to modern astronomers who believe they are similar in structure to the dust which orbited the Sun, in a similar pattern, and formed the planets some 4.5 billion years ago.

This, and other Cassini-related discoveries, were discussed at a meeting of the American Astronomical Society's division of planetary sciences on Monday.

Family dog missing after protecting kids from bear

A boxer is missing in Westmoreland County, Pennsylvania, after it chased off a bear to protect three children. According to Bill Rusko, the father of two of the children, the bear crossed Route 30 in Ligonier Township and moved towards the three kids as they played badminton. The year-old dog, Major, then ran around the bear to distract it and bit it in the face. As the bear ran back into the woods, the dog chased it. It remains missing; however, neighbors say they saw it in the area. Major is now safe at his home.

Broadband users kicked off service for constant questioning

AUK ISP, Plusnet, terminated the service of two of their broadband service customers for asking too many repeated questions and taking up too much customer support time on their portal discussion forums. Early last year, Plusnet, an ISP with nearly 200,000 subscribers, cut its prices for all of its broadband products. In doing so, Plusnet allegedly did not inform its existing customers by e-mail, and instead published new products and prices on their public portal. This manner of notice for the price changes may have resulted in thousands of customers paying almost twice as much for the same service. Within the last month, Plusnet began Packet Shaping peer-to-peer transfers for users of its 'Premier' service, which is sold and described as a 'clean' connection.

They also recently introduced the throttling [enforcing a maximum limit] of customers using more than 150GB per month of bandwidth. Users whose bandwidth is throttled receive service of 70Kbps, while paying for 2Mbps. This figure is based on the PlusNet network contention of 30:1, being 2mb divided by thirty users. The throttle is in place until the end of the customers current billing period, and is meant to help keep broadband access for all Plusnet users fast by stopping a small percentage of users from using excessive bandwidth. As a result, the ISP has begun receiving numbers of customer complaints and criticism both privately and through their publicly accessible member discussion forums. Though the vast majority of comments on this new Sustainable Usage Policy have been positive. Wade Woverly, 20, from Leeds (also known as "Wadev1589"), started a discussion in the Plusnet member discussion forums challenging the ISP on a number of customer service issues. One of those was regarding the customers who were paying an unnecessary premium for the same internet connection. In addition, Woverly mentioned he was assisting the Trading Standards Institute with an investigation of the legality of terms and conditions of Plusnet.

The accusations by Woverly, that customers are being over-charged, are considered speculative. Woverly asked the same questions dozens of times on forum pages, hoping to receive some sort of answer from Plusnet that he considered satisfactory. Ultimately, he claims the ISP called him on the telephone and said that if he didn't stop posting comments on their forums, they would terminate his ADSL internet connection and forum access. Woverly said Plusnet's position was that he was using up excessive customer services resources. After a night of lengthy posts both on Plusnet boards and at the forums at ADSLGuide, a Customer Services Manager at Plusnet, Carol Axe, allegedly contacted Woverly to inform him that they would be terminating his service, and that he has 30 days to migrate away until his line will be disconnected. Axe refused to allow her conversation to be recorded: "her voice was that of rude arrogance, not listening at all, it was a true ultimatum of a call," according to Woverly. Neil Armstrong, the Head of Marketing at Plusnet, commented, "Our comms team is there to serve all our customers, not to be drained by one unreasonably demanding customer. The Plusnet forums are led by a team of moderators, also customers, whose job it is to deal with problem posters, amongst other things. Forum Moderator Liam Martin, another stirrer, said "Part of our moderation involves restricting access to those users causing problems... and this is always carried out at our discretion when we believe somebody is causing a nuisance and/or breaking forum rules. "Wadev1589" didn't come close to being banned, in my book. This has come as a complete shock."

A second user, "pr100" from Wargrove, has since then had his service ended after being given the same ultimatum. He was told that it was "in his best interests". He responded on the Plusnet forum, "I did suggest to her that perhaps PlusNet should allow me to decide what will be my best interest whereupon she stopped beating around the bush and said that my account was being terminated because of my anti-PlusNet posts in the forum." Not all ISP's would give you the option of migrating or losing your BB connection, some would just use their right to end your contract forthwith. Another forum user, "chullbears", commented, "Carol [Axe] is in a position where she should be someone where she should be issuing an apology over this entire situation."

First encyclopedic dictionary of the Black Sea released

A new work has been just added to the list of the works on Turkey that have been made in recent years including the genres of folklore, travel, monography and encyclopedia. "Encyclopedic Dictionary of Black Sea" by Özhan Öztürk is also a first of its field. Etymological explanations are also given for the articles in the encyclopedic dictionary that is a product of work with both original resources and rather rich bibliographies. Encyclopedic Dictionary of Blacksea, a source for many answers on the Black Sea region of Anatolia, Anatolia, and is a work of a great labor. The dictionary is being published by Heyamola Publications and printed only in limited numbers. It can be a scientific resource for those who are interested in the history, culture and folklore of Black Sea. The number of the encyclopedia evaluates his work of 1260 pages.

"I don't know why no archeological excavations have been made in the Pontic coast of Anatolia. Querying why no excavations have been made in such a region that has a dense settlement as mentioned in Anabasis of Xenophon (B.C 401) is not the subject of this book. However, undoubtedly it will not be an optimistic experience to see that less excavations have been made here than in Crimea and Colchis. Another interesting and discuss-worthy issue is why arealistic analysis of the original names of villages and quarters, used by the people even after the changes of the names in Republic era, is not been made in works of the region's culture and history, including studies in Turkish. Limiting myself to cities as Ordu, Giresun, Trabzon, Rize and Artvin, I worked on original words, idioms and toponyms used by Turkish dialect speakers, independent from their native language. I made comparisons with vernaculars from surrounding cities including Samsun, Erzurum and Gümüşhane, Anatolia, and from some surrounding countries. I hope that the comparison of the original toponyms with equivalents from Anatolia, Greece/Hellas, Armenia, Georgia, Azerbaijan and other Turkish states could be useful for those interested in regional history, and influential for researchers."

While some village names in regions do match with the villages names in Crete and Epirus, no equivalents are found in Anatolia and Northern Hellas. Some village names akin to those in Northern Abkhazia, the motherland of Laz, show remnants of Pelasgi and Thracians, the population of Anatolia and Hellas, prior to the Indo-Europeans. This requires a re-examination not only of Anatolian and regional history, but also of the history of a wider area, ranging from the Caucasus to the Balkans.

Volcanic bulge found in Oregon

As they have done for the last four years, United States Geological Survey (USGS) scientists were measuring an approximate 100 square mile bulge in central Oregon near the South Sister this past August. The bulge is located 25 miles outside of the city of Bend, Ore. and three miles from the South Sister. The results of this years survey won't be available for some weeks, but geologists have come to some conclusions based on the past four years of monitoring. The initial discovery was made by using information from the European Space Agency's (ESA) Interferometric Satellite Aperture Radar satellite. Scientists believe the bulge is rising at a rate of 1.4 inches per year and is due to a large lake of fluid (likely magma) that is 4.5 miles below the surface. They also think the fluid covers an area about one mile across and extends to a depth of 65 feet. The pooling fluid could be shifting magma or the creation of a new volcano. Ground swells aren't an extraordinary occurrence in geology. Geologists suspect that these ground swellings occur in the Cascade Range and at other volcanoes, and the majority of them do not lead to eruptions. Using the same ESA satellite technology, geologists have seen lots of bulges in the Aleutian Islands that have not lead to eruptions.

United States government hiring more hackers

At a hackers conference in Las Vegas with the spoofed name of Defcon, the Assistant Secretary of Defense Linton Wells made a pitch to attendees: "If you want to work on cutting-edge problems, if you want to be part of the truly great issues of our time ... we invite you to work with us." Technology commentator Richard Thieme said that there are many Feds attending undercover; "You can't be deceived by the uniforms. I talked at the Pentagon, and one-third of the people in the audience I already knew from Defcon." Attendees who "out" the undercover ops are awarded free "I" shirts. A "Meet the Feds" panel was attended by a man who demanded, "I would like to know why the federal government, especially some of the law enforcement agencies, are destroying this country." Pentagon people would not comment on the rumours that they are looking for people to attack "foreign" networks. "I'm learning while I'm here but I'm also getting the names of people," said Don Blumenthal of the Federal Trade Commission. The Feds arrested a Russian programmer Dmitry Sklyarov at the annual 2001 Defcon conference. The gathering is attended by computer security experts, hackers and crackers of all types who celebrate the cutting edge of the technology.

Archaeologists find 1.8M-year-old Homo erectus skull in Georgia
The oldest such skull to be found in Europe

Archaeologists say they have found a 1.8 million-year-old Homo erectus skull in Georgia, the oldest such skull to be found in Europe. According to David Lordkipanidze, director of the Georgian National Museum, the skull was found August 6 and excavated on August 21 in Dmanisi, about 85 km southwest of Tbilisi. The skull was said to have been found at a site archaeologists have been examining since 1936 along with four other bones and fragments, including a jaw bone found in 1991. "Practically all the remains have been found in one place.

This indicates that we have found a place of settlement of primitive people," said Lordkipanidze.[1]

The researchers said their outside Africa. The skull and other remains have been cited as evidence of Homo erectus's migration into Europe at least 500,000 years earlier than has previously been thought.

Fossils of the hominid ancestor have been found in Africa, the Middle East, and Asia. Some of Lordkipanidze's earlier findings that made them slender, small features, including a smaller brain relative to Homo sapiens, contradicted anthropological theories that Homo erectus was large and intelligent even by Homo sapiens standards.

Best if served by:

Fresh fish served daily

LEGAL SEA FOODS

If it isn't fresh, it isn't Legal.

ASKING THE RIGHT KIND OF QUESTIONS

Keep analysing the product, the project or the problem until you've dug out its deepest secrets. Be as inquisitive as a child, but stay focused on the goal and as obsessed with detail as a hotshot attorney.

The most essential tool when formulating your goal is asking the right questions. Questions lead to answers, and unusual but appropriate questions can lead to unusual but appropriate answers. As we have already seen in previous chapters, questions steer the discussion and can even steer your client's imagination. For instance, you might ask what would happen if suddenly the number of women shopping in a hardware store increased by 70 per cent. The client would first have to visualize the scene, then the consequences, and then would have to decide whether or not the new situation would have a significant impact on the present one. It would mean comparing a future hypothesis to present reality, and then gauging any changes that would have to be made. In a moment I will suggest three lines of questioning that you will need to cover before you can formulate your goal. You could start the conversation with a few questions to circumscribe the problem that lies hidden in the heart of the project. The deeper you delve, the more clearly you will see what other questions need to be asked. Even with these indirect questions, however, you must

proceed logically so that the information you have gained won't get tangled up in a confused mess. Maintain an overview, focus on the questions, keep probing, and categorize the information. Think of it as a cross-examination, and never lose sight of the fact that you have a particular aim in mind. The three lines of questioning offer an almost infinite variety of possibilities that will enable you to get closer and closer to the creative goal, and ultimately to find exactly the right phrasing to convey it.

▶ What is the problem?
Just ask every question that can help you get to the bottom of it: what's the cause, who is involved, what will be the consequences if you can't solve it, does it have a positive side, what's been done so far to cope with the difficulties?

▶ What is the goal?
During the briefing, stick rigidly to this topic and make sure that every question takes you closer to a clear formulation. What is the goal, is there more than

one, and if so, which of them should you tackle first? Can the project be described in more concrete detail? If the central goal is unattainable, is there an alternative? Is there an ulterior motive hidden behind the goal? How will you know when the goal has actually been reached?

▶ Is the information based on facts or assumptions? This question will tell you quickly and simply about the quality of the answers you have been given. People often try to sell you their assumptions or intuitive guesses as facts, so test their statements by repeating the above question.

Client Volkswagen | Agency DDB

Golf R32. Perfectly tuned.

Talking point: What needs to be changed in your firm to ensure that questions are seen as an inspirational source of ideas rather than a necessary chore? Your creative team especially should try to think of unusual questions that might lead to original campaigns like the one above.

▲ **Strategy:** By rearranging musical instruments creatively, this print campaign takes the idea of tuning an engine literally.

THE GOAL BEHIND THE GOAL

Our perception of a city changes when we climb a hill and see a full panorama instead of a narrow street view. Everything becomes much clearer when you can see the bigger context.

Imagine a man comes into a bookshop and asks for a book on fitness. Could there be an ulterior motive behind the inquiry? Is he really after the book, or something quite different? If you had the chance to ask him a couple of unusual questions before selling him the book, you might receive answers something like these:

Bookseller: What do you expect to get from buying this book?
Customer: I might feel like taking up sport again.
Bookseller: And what would you get from doing sport?
Customer: I might go to a fitness centre.
Bookseller: And what do you expect to get from going to a fitness centre?
Customer: I'd start mixing with people again.
Bookseller: And what would you get from mixing with people?
Customer: I'd make more contacts.
Bookseller: And what would be the point of making more contacts?
Customer: Well, then I might have a chance of meeting a nice girl.
Bookseller: Why do you want to meet a nice girl?

Customer: I've been living on my own for years in a great big house.
Bookseller: What would you get from not being alone in your great big house?
Customer: It would be nice to start a family.
Bookseller: And what would you get from starting a family?
Customer: I'd be happy!

Many projects have what we might call a meta-goal, or a goal behind the goal. It isn't always vital to know what that is, but it can sometimes help us to get a better understanding of the project, product, strategy, target group or the clients themselves. If you're clever enough to root out the meta-goal, it will give you a quicker route to the right strategy or formulation that you can present to your team. It's a process that opens up a broader context as well as revealing the true motivation behind various actions and attitudes. For instance, the focus might be on a target group. Let's say you're working on an online campaign for eBay; it would be useful to seek out the meta-goal that makes people take part in an online auction. This might be especially helpful if you want to know why people tend to overbid on some days and underbid on others. Apart from the obvious one of picking up a bargain, are there are other reasons for taking part in an auction? There is another context, too, in which recognizing the meta-goal can be very helpful: during the briefing meeting with the client. What, for instance, might lie behind the aim of informing the public about the dangers of smoking? Supposing the Ministry of Health commissions you to produce an anti-smoking campaign, but then they reject every single proposal.

Perhaps you believe that they want a really effective campaign, and you're offering them powerful ideas which might shock people or polarize public opinion. However, it may be that the Ministry simply wants to give voters the impression that they are concerned about the nation's health, but they don't really care about the subject itself. Maybe it's pre-election time, and politicians want to show their best side, but they don't want to upset voters or cause any controversy. This kind of campaign is a means to a hidden end.

▲ Strategy: For their 'Loads of Hope' campaign, Tide transformed a truck into a launderette, filled with 32 energy-saving washing machines. Since 2005, they have done this regularly in regions of the USA that have been hit by natural disasters. Tide CleanStart has now helped more than 20,000 families in need by washing their clothes for free.

Talking point: What are the goals of this campaign, and which of them has priority? What are the public aims, and what are the less obvious aims? Goals that do not appear in the brief are often extremely important and are vigorously pursued by some people. How can the creative team be made aware of them so that they don't have a negative influence on the creative process?

▲ **Strategy:** 'The Art of the Motorcycle', an exhibition at the Guggenheim Museum in Bilbao.

Talking point: What would be the goal of a project like this, according to the brief? What other aims might be involved that are not mentioned in the brief, although they might have a big influence on the success of the project? What are the goals of the press officer and of the board of directors, what personal and political goals might also play a role, and what is the goal in relation to the target group? It is the account handler's task to ask questions that will reach beyond the 'official' goal, so that the project can be designed accordingly.

FAST-TRACK CONSUMER INSIGHT: LOOK INSIDE YOURSELF

Can you picture being able to understand the behaviour of consumers even before they understand it themselves? Look inside yourself, be brutally honest, and sometimes you will learn more than your consumers would ever be willing to divulge about themselves.

Consumer insight is a concept that's long been used in advertising and marketing but has rarely been given a precise definition. Ideally, it's supposed to give agency creatives an insight into the motives, emotions and behavioural patterns of the target group regarding a product or brand. Consumer insight also has a great deal of influence on the formulated goals that creative teams use to develop ideas for campaigns. It can open up surprising new perspectives that go way beyond the stale clichés and superficial stereotypes that block the path to originality. The only problem is how to obtain this insight. In most cases it's hidden within private thoughts and ideas that no one would want to share with market researchers or focus groups. If the topic is one that people don't mind talking about, the exercise often fails because interviewees doesn't really have a strong stance on it. Or it may be that they'll say one thing, and do another. They'll tell you, cigarette in hand, that smoking is bad for their health. Or they'll declare that exercise is essential, when they haven't set foot in a gym for years. In other words, they'll give you the answer they think is socially acceptable. False assessments that underlie the introduction of new products, ad campaigns and even elections show just how difficult the job of agency creatives really is.

The cheapest and quickest way to gain consumer insight is through introspection. This what I call fast-track consumer insight. The fact is that you and I are clients, consumers, and members of target groups ourselves. The only precondition for this exercise is that you must be totally honest with yourself. You'd like an example? All right, here is a question: In the last five years, have you ever watched a porn film? Now I hope you've been honest with yourself, because the chances are good that you would have given me a different answer to the one you gave yourself. Another example: how do you behave when you're alone at home munching a packet of potato crisps? And how do you behave when you're at a friend's house? What would you do if your friend left you alone in the room for ten minutes with the last ten crisps in the packet? What would go through your head, and how would you cope with your thoughts? If you're honest, you'll admit that only under certain conditions would you tell the whole truth: either you'd answer these questions silently to yourself, or you'd be sitting with friends you've known for ever and trust completely.

The really interesting consumer insights generally transcend the rules and regulations, conventions and customs that are accepted by our society. With this in mind, it can actually be a lot of fun to work with insights into products such as crisps. What would you do if you found they were stale? Do you take your crisps out of the packet one by one, or in handfuls? Do you take enough to last you for a while, or do you have faith that other people will leave you enough for a second helping? Do you take the packet off the table and then see how the other guests react? How do you put the crisps into your mouth? Even more interesting, how do you eat them when you think no one is watching? The list of questions is endless, and honest answers can lead to surprising revelations as well as excellent raw material for new ideas. The first step towards fast-track consumer insight is to engage a small team of people who enjoy a bit of fun, have complete confidence in one another, and in due course will build up an atmosphere in which no one is afraid to tell stories that go against all our social standards and taboos.

Credits From a TV ad for Reebok | Illustrator Max Julian Otto

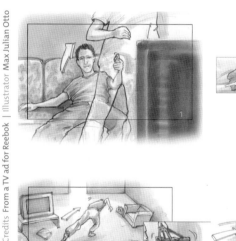
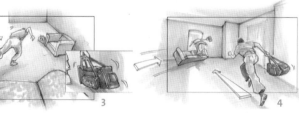

◄ **Strategy:** In this TV ad, a bored young man is lounging around watching TV. When eventually he switches off the TV and moves to get up, the sofa jerks back underneath him and forces him to flop back down again. This sets off a mighty struggle between man and sofa. When he sees a chance to get away, he grabs his Reebok bag and rushes towards the door. But the sofa is too quick for him and again prevents his escape. It pulls him back into the room by his leg, and all his efforts to resist are thwarted. Finally, he manages to flee downstairs, and the sofa comes tumbling after him, but in its attempt to catch him it gets stuck in a doorway. The man emerges victorious from the battle, proudly picks up his bag, and hurries out of the house to head for the playing field. 'Escape the sofa. Reebok.'

Talking point: You don't always get the best material from a direct approach to the target group. If you want to get to the bottom of riskier subjects, it's best to slip into the shoes of your customers. Find out for yourself what they think and feel, and how they live their lives.

HOW CREATIVITY ADDS VALUE AND MEANING

The creative industries can turn a fruit into an international brand (Apple) or a mediocre singer into a pop superstar (TV talent shows). The art of adding value is one of the finest there is.

Many brands are so weak or commonplace that they have very little chance of survival on the market. Branding teams face the challenge of loading products with values and meanings which at first glance simply don't exist. Without a USP, benefit or reason to believe, it's usually difficult to work out a convincing goal to help the creative team develop a successful marketing approach. What is needed is a preliminary phase – before the goal is formulated – in which the team meets to generate ideas for giving the product a slant that people will regard as useful or valuable. There shouldn't be more than four people at this meeting, and for 40 to 50 minutes they should think of as many new and surprising angles as possible. I'd like to suggest five different approaches that we might call reframings. Reframing is a way of looking at objects, situations, statements or people from an unusual perspective. For instance, you can place them in different contexts. The statement 'That's enough!' will mean something quite different if it's applied to buying cake, or to a heated exchange between two politicians. In the first instance, it's positive, and in the second negative. The following sample ads will illustrate just how these different approaches work. Of course their use is not simply confined to advertising: they can be applied to the development of new products and services, or the finding of new uses for existing products, thereby adding value.

Get them off your dog.

FRONTLINE
FLEA & TICK SPRAY
available at JAKPETZ

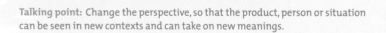

▲ Strategy: This oversized image creates a playful change of perspective. Seen from above, people in the lobby look like fleas.

Talking point: Change the perspective, so that the product, person or situation can be seen in new contexts and can take on new meanings.

SLIM & LITE

PSP

PlayStation.Portable

PURSUIT

por sólo
199,99€
Imposible separarse de ella

Talking point: In what surroundings might the product take on a different meaning? In what situation could it be used in a surprising way?

▲ **Strategy:** This print ad shows the inescapable lure of the Sony PlayStation Portable.

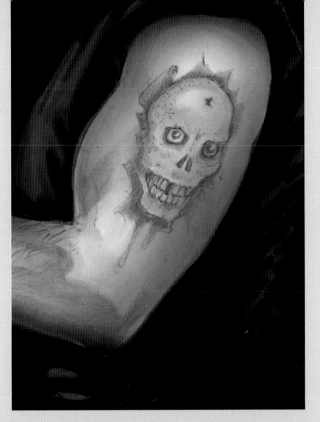

THINK OF IT AS A DO NOT DISTURB SIGN.

BENNO'S TATTOOING.

◄ **Strategy:** A striking way to attract customers to a tattoo studio.

Talking point: Consider changing the name of the product in order to extend its meaning, value or use.

► **Strategy:** Ad for Wrigley's Extra sugar-free chewing gum.

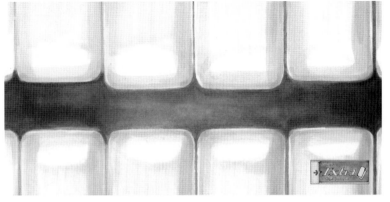

Talking point: What double meanings can the appearance, name or use of a product be given in order to increase its appeal?

◄ **Strategy:** Shopping malls often feature floor lights that are shaped rather like the front window of a washing machine. Tide placed a simplified image of a washing machine around the light to illustrate the extraordinary brightness you get from using their washing powder.

Client Procter & Gamble | Agency Leo Burnett

Talking point: What else could a product or object be combined with, in order to give it a new meaning or a surprising use?

GO RIGHT TO THE SOURCE TO WATCH AND LEARN

The rules of the game: one player whispers a piece of information to another player, who whispers it to the next person in line, and so on. The fun comes from the fact that the last person in the line has to announce the whispered message out loud. The more accidental changes the original message undergoes, the louder the laughter at the end.

The game of 'Chinese Whispers' or 'Telephone' is not just a popular game for children but is also played by many agency creatives when they're developing projects. The path from the source of the problem to the ears and minds of those who are to solve it is often tortuous and tedious. For example, if a research institute doing a project on nanotechnology is planning to present its findings at an international trade fair, it may well happen that up to six different people are involved in passing on the information before it finally gets to the creative team. The more people who handle the information, the more gaps and distortions there are likely to be by the time of the briefing. There are several reasons why it makes sense for there to be direct communication between the problemmakers and problem-solvers. First-hand information is more emotionally engaged and more authentic than information passed on second- or third-hand. A good rule of thumb here is what I call the MacGyver

principle. This TV action hero never gets a written brief, but no matter where a problem arises, he's always in the thick of things, and 100 per cent committed to finding the answer on the spot. He takes the shortest possible route from problem to solution. For a creative team, it's generally enough if they can experience the problem at its source, and watch and listen quietly in order to absorb all the information they'll need to find the right solution. If you haven't witnessed for yourself that visitors are leaving a particular stand after just 20 seconds, you'll find it much harder to work out how to keep them there for longer. If you haven't watched customers browsing in a shoe shop, how can you possibly know what might grab their attention and maintain it? And if you've never spent any time in a supermarket to observe shoppers taking a packet off the shelf to have a closer look, you'll hardly be in a position to design attractive product packaging.

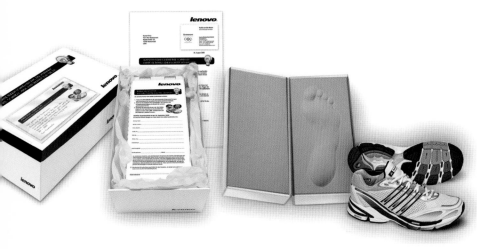

Client **Lenovo** | Agency agencyteam Stuttgart GmbH

◀ **Strategy:** The IT company Lenovo prides itself on its efficient products at competitive prices, as well as its prompt, on-the-spot service. To convey their trademark philosophy, they sent out a shoebox with a foam pad on which receivers could leave an imprint of their foot. This was collected, and within a very short time a Lenovo representative came back with a pair of made-to-measure sneakers, along with information on Lenovo's range of services.

Talking point: It's not enough these days just to know the product – you also have to know what customers do with it. As a creative, you should think of yourself as a voyeur, studying the intimate relationship between product and consumer. The closer you get to them, the more interesting your ideas will be. Follow the customers from the moment of purchase to the moment of use, so that you'll understand what makes the relationship click.

▶ **Strategy:** The launch of the luxury liner *AIDAdiva* in Hamburg was accompanied by a spectacular firework display and light show.

Client AIDA Cruises | Agency PROCON Event Engineering GmbH

Talking point: Before an event, send a creative team to the location so that they can use all their senses in experiencing the product. Leave a second team back at the office and show them photos of the product and the location. Then send both teams to separate meetings. Which of them do you think will end up with the more emotionally engaging and exciting ideas?

▲ **Strategy:** The Kymyka shoe shop in Maastricht displays its range of shoes like colourful butterflies perching on steel posts. The shoes are held in position by powerful magnets.

Talking point: Develop ideas that will get customers to take shoes in their hands, and so feel the unique qualities of the different styles. Then spend a few days in shoe shops to see when and how customers pick up the shoes, what they actually do with their hands, whether both arms are always free, if there's a crush at the shelves, at what level people are most likely to reach for the shoes, and how they put them back. If you've seen all these things for yourself, you are halfway to solving the problem.

ARE YOUR IDEAS AIMED AT THE CLIENT OR THE TARGET GROUP?

*'I said to my dad, "I am just one good idea
away from starting my own venture."
My dad answered, "No, what you need
is not an idea, it's a customer."'*

Sarah Nowlin

The basic mission of the creative industries is to come up with ideas that will strongly appeal to the target group – and not necessarily to their own department or even to the client. For some people, however, as time goes by it's the clients who take priority. And so, dear reader, if you are a client and one day you happen to notice that certain creatives are trying to come up with ideas that they think you'll like, put an immediate end to your relationship with them. They are in the process of ruining your business. It would seem that their only concern is to please you and to satisfy your personal tastes with their made-to-measure ideas, and they have totally forgotten about the people that your business is supposed to be targeting. If you're the boss and you have a marketing director who behaves in the same way, get rid of him too – and do it now! He is also ruining your business. If you run a business yourself and are reading this text, then the next time you meet a creative director, bear in mind that you are not the target group but the client. Always remember that at the end of the day, it's the fish and not the angler that has to swallow the worm.

Client Tzabar Travel Agency | Agency Grey

▶ **Strategy:** Tzabar Tours offers a package deal consisting of flight and tickets for concerts by international stars.

Talking point: Creative work like this can often lead to fierce controversy among the creative team, the client, and sometimes even the public. If you try to please all of the people all of the time, you'll fail. But if you always keep the relevant target group in mind, your campaign has a much better chance of success.

◀ **Strategy:**
Belgian TV channel PLUG TV always does its own thing, with a wide variety of programming including strange cult series, an unusual music show, and a relentless breaking of taboos. Its stings and idents are bold and original and it is always looking for new ways of breaking away from TV conventions.

Talking point: With a project like this, how would you keep reminding your team of the target group they are trying to impress with their ideas?

▶ **Strategy:** The PODLE™ pocket spray is designed to hold perfumes and other cosmetics. Its patented locking system makes it secure and easy for travellers to handle.

Talking point: During discussions within the team or involving the client, there should be a rule determining whether ideas are to be judged according to subjective taste or according to their relevance to the target group. Everyone concerned needs to draw a clear line between these two forms of judgment.

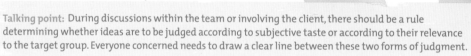

When people confuse design with ideas or concepts, the result is an elaborate illusion that hides the fact that there is no clear goal. The two groups that are particularly susceptible to this phenomenon are clients and agencies.

Many creative works are so good to look at that observers have no choice but to rave over them. But what was the message that the campaign was supposed to convey, and what were the thoughts and actions it was intended to spark off? What was the goal of the event, website, packaging or trade stand? When beautiful design becomes an end in itself, and goal-orientated ideas get left behind, something has gone very wrong. Sometimes design is the lowest common denominator between client and agency when they fail to develop a clear strategy, and then the idea fades into the background and the dazzling lure of aesthetics takes over. In the end, both parties are happy, and even the target group is sometimes impressed, but that's not enough if the aim is communication or sales. Of course, great design is good for a brand, but if there's no concrete target, message or strategy, the exercise will be futile. This may be illustrated by an example from the field of product design: imagine a superb-looking designer chair that everyone loves – until they actually sit on it. It may be so uncomfortable that you can't stay put for more than three minutes. The American architect Louis Sullivan summed it up perfectly: 'Form follows function.' This became a watchword for all designers, because design must be derived from the goal of the object. In some branches of the creative industries, this principle is not so clear as in product design or architecture – for instance, in communications it may not be immediately obvious that the envelope looks great but the message has become lost on the way. Unfortunately, in advertising you may not find out until it's too late.

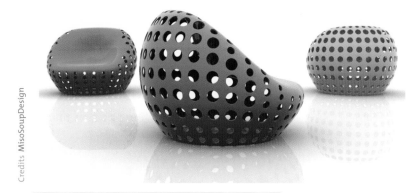

▲ **Strategy:** By including connections for lamps, speakers or music players, the pOrOus designer chair allows users to create their own atmosphere. The chair is made from recycled polyester.

Talking point: The principle of 'form follows function' is not as obvious in all the products of the creative industries as it is in the design of these chairs. How can you test whether campaigns, websites or events have replaced the function and goal with design?

▶ **Strategy:** The Petit Jardin chair is laser-cut from galvanized steel and painted white. But to find out whether it really makes you feel as if you're sitting in a garden full of flowers, you really need to test it for yourself.

► Strategy:
'Fashion for Walls.'

FASHION FOR WALLS
by Levis Ambiance

Talking point: This ad looks great, and has a clear goal. How could you
use a print campaign to show that Levis covers walls in the finest paints?

The creative process begins and ends with the team leader. The person who approved the formulated goal should also be there at the presentation and should take part in the selection of the right idea.

If the clients have put together the brief and set out a strategy, then they should work with the agency to establish one or more clearly formulated goals. These goals should define in a simple and straightforward way what is expected of the creatives in relation to this commission. For instance, for a sports shop, what facilities can we provide to allow customers to test the equipment on the premises? The clients should then put their signature to the formulated goal, to show that they are jointly responsible for the strategy and that its aims are binding on all parties. This process is crucial for both the clients and the agency. If it isn't followed, you can bet that at some point in the process, someone will deny responsibility, in which case the seeds of failure were sown right at the start. In the final presentation phase it is equally essential that the person who agreed to the formulated goal should also take part in the selection process. If we see the goal as a question that the client is asking the creatives, then the ideas at the presentation are the creatives' answer to the client. Would it make any sense to give someone an answer unless they know the question first? This would only lead to confusion, and making a fair judgment would be almost impossible since a key piece of the necessary information would be missing.

Client Moroso | Agency Studio Arne Quinze

▲ **Strategy:** 'Caged Beauty', a trade stand for the Italian furniture brand Moroso, combines simplicity with fragile complexity. A dense web of fibreglass, lit from above, forms delicate boxes inside which the products seem to float.

Talking point: The ideas presented to a client are, in an ideal scenario, answers to the question asked by the formulated goal. How can you make it an integral feature of the creative process that, from the very beginning, all parties including the directors are fully conversant with the goal, so that there need be no nasty surprises at the presentation phase?

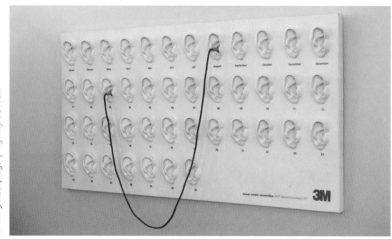

Client 3M Earplugs | Agency BUTTER.

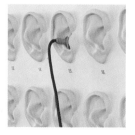

◄ **Strategy:** This calendar reminds 3M customers throughout the year how simple it is to use their new earplugs to shut out unwanted noise.

CREATIVE PROCESS

05

Idea management is a process that gives a creative department the space it needs to fulfil up to 99 per cent of its potential. It focuses on countering the usual creative chaos, contingencies or premature demise of interesting ideas with a truly effective mode of working.

When a promising idea bites the dust, it can often be because it was left to intuition alone instead of being passed through a systematic creative process. After more than fifteen years of working with teams from throughout the creative industries, I have developed a creative process which has been remarkably effective in day-to-day use, producing great ideas with a significantly higher chance of success. In the pages that follow, I shall explain how this process can be put into operation, in order to raise both the standard of ideas and the standard of results. The ten separate points show the sequence of stages that successful teams work through. I'd like to invite any teams that feel they don't need idea management to analyse some of their best ideas in detail, so that perhaps afterwards they can find out which factors have led to success. I think they will find that generally, behind what may sometimes appear to be luck, the best ideas almost always pass through the phases listed opposite. There are two vital factors to be borne in mind here: first, the phases are separate, and second, they must take place in strict sequence. If you take a look at ideas or projects ranging from mediocre to disastrous, you will soon notice that certain key phases have been skipped or at least rushed. It makes no difference whether a team does or doesn't know how idea management functions; the best projects will still have followed this scheme. The difference, however, will be that teams who consciously set out to use this method can save themselves a lot of time, money and nervous energy.

1. *First client briefing*

   ↓

2. *Problem identification and analysis*

   ↓

3. *Goal formulation and strategy*

   ↓

4. *Research and knowledge management*

   ↓

5. *Collection of raw materials*

   ↓

6. *Idea development*

   ↓

7. *Preliminary presentation*

   ↓

8. *Idea evaluation*

   ↓

9. *Presentation*

   ↓

10. *Implementation*

Client Microsoft | Agency Chugg Entertainment, Pulse Communications, Triangle Communications, Rinsed Studio

▲ **Strategy:** The new generation of Xbox 360 games consoles was launched on Coogee Beach in Australia with the biggest beachball fight in the world. More than 2,800 gamers and fans from all over the world took part in this fun event.

Talking point: Which of the ten points of the creative process would you have to leave out or swap around in order to mess up or totally ruin this unusual idea?

▲ **Strategy:** This print campaign uses exaggeration to illustrate the unmatchable strength of Kleenex kitchen towels.

Talking point: The secret to regularly producing original ideas such as this one generally lies in an awareness of which steps need to be taken in which order. If you compare the process with baking a cake, what would happen if you threw flour, sugar and all the other ingredients straight into the oven, took it all out after 30 minutes, emptied it into a cake tin and then stirred it for 15 minutes?

IDEA MANAGEMENT IS A SERIOUS BUSINESS

A great idea depends on 50 % information, 49 % method, and 1 % inspiration. The oft-quoted 99% perspiration will happen in its own time!

Thomas Edison famously said: 'Genius is one per cent inspiration and ninety-nine per cent perspiration.' In the creative industries, which probably produce several million ideas a year, Edison's equation is not entirely true. If 1 % inspiration was enough in the old days, the competitive modern world requires a great deal more in the shape of idea management skills. Let me say it again: idea management is a radical and serious business. Just knowing the rules but not sticking to them simply won't work. It's like football: the rules provide a framework, and within those parameters, teams can create an infinite number of original variations. In creative projects, teams that don't know the rules may already have failed during the first third of the process, because they confuse the different phases and don't actually know where they stand in relation to the process as a whole. Suddenly they'll start asking questions about the brief when they're meant to be developing ideas, or reformulating goals with the client during the implementation phase, or talking about implementation when they haven't collected any raw ideas yet. The result will be chaos. One thing is clear: under circumstances like these, good ideas will only emerge by chance, and the general standard will never rise above mediocrity. A smidgeon of idea management will not suffice. Creative teams and agency directors need to work together to give this process the most solid foundation possible, moving systematically from phase to phase, in order to create radical and serious change.

▲ Strategy: The '100 Yards for People with No Sense of Direction' – a Monty Python sketch – offers a humorous view of what can happen when teams stick to the rules at the start, but then mistake lack of focus and structure for creative freedom.

Credits From the Monty Python 'Silly Olympiad' sketch | Illustrator Max Julian Otto

Client Outline Innovation B.V. | Creatives Jens Andersson, Jonas Forsman

◄ Strategy: 'Wine in a Can' is an award-winning packaging design that offers travellers good-quality wine without the need for a corkscrew, glasses or a breakable bottle. The neat aluminium can lets you enjoy your wine just as much as if you were drinking from a glass.

Talking point: Before they can be put into practice, ideas like this can run into all sorts of problems. In order to maintain the quality of the idea, and not dilute it drop by drop with a series of compromises, you must stick radically to the structures of the creative process, seeking the best possible solution at each stage.

▶ **Strategy:** The Prada Transformer was designed by the architect Rem Koolhaas, and is a building unlike any other. It is 20 metres (65 feet) high and weighs 180 tonnes, but it can be turned and rolled like a dice. Each of its surfaces can act as a wall, ceiling or floor. Located in the centre of Seoul, the Transformer has been used for a fashion exhibition, a runway couture show, an art exhibit and a film festival, and for each of these events it was moved into a different position.

Client Prada | Agency OMA

Talking point: What would you have to do in order to prevent your team from taking a complex project like this one from start to finish?

THE CREATIVE PROCESS AS A PLAYGROUND FOR ORIGINALITY

The uniqueness of an idea often derives from the uniqueness of the person who developed it. If you try to force that person into a standard method of working, you will risk getting nothing but standard results.

Anyone who has been in close contact with creatives will know that most of them are individualists in thought and action. The unusual nature of their ideas is usually matched by the unusual nature of their personalities and working methods. Some need absolute peace and quiet in order to work on their ideas, whereas others welcome stimulation from outside, and want to engage their colleagues in intensive discussions. Some sit absolutely still during the quest for ideas, and others pace nervously up and down. Pressure from outside can be an inspiration, or it can lead to complete blockage. If you fail to meet these different requirements, you will fail to promote creativity. Idea management requires a clearly structured procedure, but it does not mean stopping people from doing things their own way. On the contrary, everyone should be encouraged to find out for themselves what working conditions will lead to the best results. Interestingly, you will frequently find that the majority of people don't even know when, where or how they get their best ideas. And yet at a basic level, all creatives ought to know exactly what they need in order to do their jobs. One useful step in the right direction is self-observation while you work, so that you can gauge for yourself what conditions bring forth your best ideas.

Another way of identifying the parameters is to think back and recall three situations in which you reached your creative peak. Work out what factors played a key role on those occasions. For instance, it may be that in all three a decisive factor was a relaxed atmosphere in sheltered surroundings. Or perhaps you were inspired by magazines, books or websites. Here are a few of the factors that can influence people's working habits and hence their results:

► Switching quickly between administrative and creative tasks
► Developing ideas on your own or in a team
► Developing ideas in quiet surroundings or with stimulus from outside
► Pressure versus relaxation
► Lots of information or a lack of it
► Work versus play
► Working on one project or several at the same time
► Vague goals versus clear goals

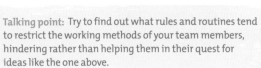

Client Rémy Cointreau | Agency Sleever International

◄ **Strategy:** The fashion designers Viktor & Rolf were commissioned by renowned French champagne makers Piper Heidsieck to design a complete champagne set. The bottle, bucket and glasses are all designed to look as if they are standing upside down.

Talking point: Try to find out what rules and routines tend to restrict the working methods of your team members, hindering rather than helping them in their quest for ideas like the one above.

► **Strategy:** The trouble with tagged teabags is that the tag often ends up in the tea. Elisabeth Sóos's little boat turns a minor irritation into a bit of fun.

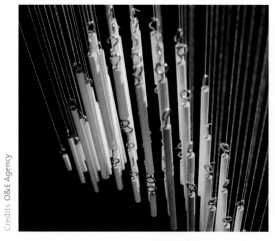

▶ **Strategy:** Each letter of this 3D text is made up of 50 wooden rods hanging on threads, and every change of angle produces a new visual effect.

Talking point: How could you encourage your team members to turn their workplace into a personalized playing field that would help them to experiment with ideas like this?

WHAT GETS SQUASHED BY TIME PRESSURES?

Do you think the best ideas emerge under pressure? Great, then work out a brilliant idea for a revolutionary exhibition in five minutes. Is that enough pressure for you? Or should we reduce the timescale even more, so that you get even better ideas?

A football match lasts 90 minutes, and no matter what happens before or after it, those 90 minutes are for playing the game and nothing else. Within those 90 minutes, there's no such thing as time pressure, because the 90 minutes stay the same, no matter what. If you follow this principle with your creative team during the idea development phase, and give them a clear time frame, it will act as a sort of haven within which they will be able to focus strictly on the task in hand. The opposite approach will lead to chaotic sessions with no real beginning or end, in which themes ranging from the brief to the implementation will get mixed up, so that the participants will feel increasingly insecure. Time pressures can occasionally be mistaken for chaos, and briefs can often be left to the last minute because it's assumed that the creative team will somehow muddle through. If clients or account handlers act in this way, it goes to show how little they know about the creative process and about what a creative team needs in order to produce the best results. Many clients still think a creative department is a sort of magical black box which can somehow produce the goods no matter what happens. You should never forget that if people are

working under pressure, they are most likely to fall back on what they know best, i.e. the old tried and trusted successes of yesteryear. In other words, they will repeat themselves. This is a psychological state that I call 'zero creativity', because in order to play safe, your team can only *re*-create, perhaps by making tiny modifications to past ideas.

If you're serious about investing in creativity, then you must seriously invest your time in it. Slow things down, to allow scope for germination and evolution. Pressure often comes either from inside the agency or from the client, and so it needs to be relieved right from the outset. Idea management means that the team should not feel helpless in the face of a client's deadlines. Instead of complaining, you should actively involve clients – especially new ones – in the whole process, so that they learn to understand the basic principles. This will also increase the sense of cooperation between both sides. If the clients have no idea how a creative team works, it's only to be expected that they will miscalculate the time needed. Supposing you go to a glazier and commission him to make windows for a church, giving him a deadline of two days including installation. Does that make you crazy?

No, it just means that you don't know any better. Here are some good reasons why you should think twice about putting your creatives under time pressure:

▶ If time is short, individuals tend to work alone rather than with their team. The result will be a production-line product, with a concomitant drop in quality.

▶ Too little time will kill creativity, but so will too much. Only someone who properly understands the creative process will be able to gauge the amount of time needed.

▶ Integrate your clients into the idea management process, so they learn how much time is needed.

▶ Use briefing workshops as a way to get a new project underway in good time, and reduce the pressures right from the start.

▶ There is only one point at which you can prevent time pressure, and that is at the very beginning of the project. This is your one and only chance to set the timetable with the client.

▶ Allocate the different tasks to the right people. Make sure that the clients are not the only ones allowed to set the timetable – this should always be worked out in collaboration with the agency.

▶ Teams can often cope surprisingly well with a certain degree of time pressure. The quality only deteriorates if working methods end up descending into chaos, and teams can no longer focus on fully developing their ideas within the time that remains.

▶ Short-term pressure can spur creatives on to new heights, but permanent pressure will only lead to creative burnout.

▲ Strategy: In this Durex TV ad, inflated condoms are turned into cute balloon animals that make passionate love in front of the camera, letting out the squeaky noises that balloons make when they rub up against each other.

Client **Durex** | Agency Fitzgerald + CO

Talking point: Time pressures often lead to teams being unable to work together, as each individual is preoccupied with meeting a separate deadline. What is lost if a team is no longer able to combine ideas or cooperate on implementing them?

▼ **Strategy:** The bookcase 'Of Wars & Wits & Power' is a political allusion to nuclear testing in North Korea. A missile-shaped case is held aloft by a 'Golden Army' which stands ready at all times to prove the country's military might.

Talking point: If an individual creative is put under time pressure, the consequences will be different from when a whole team is under pressure. What are the most common problems that arise within a team if it is exposed to unreasonable deadlines over an extended period?

DON'T BRAINSTORM — COLLECT RAW MATERIALS

If you chop down a tree, it would never occur to anyone to say that you've made a table; only in the hands of a carpenter will the wood become a piece of furniture. It therefore makes no sense for the raw ideas that emerge from brainstorming to be so often regarded as fully rounded concepts ready for implementation.

The aim of the first creative meeting should not be to brainstorm but to collect raw materials. There are good reasons for this. The moment you mention brainstorming, many people feel under pressure to come up with the perfect solution straight away. The goal of the first meeting should be to play around with the facts and figures which in due course will be built up into workable concepts, little by little. What happens in brainstorming sessions is very different. Expectations are immediately far too high, so some of those present try desperately to come up with lots of brilliant suggestions, while the rest are paralysed by indecision. The resulting list of ideas is generally too short and most of them have been seen before. The team then enters the evaluation phase, treating the ideas as if they were already fully fashioned and ready to be put into operation.

None of this makes any sense at all. The raw materials that are collected in the first session need to be seen for what they are: fragments, options, suggestions, approaches, possibilities – none of which are yet ready to be put to the reality test. Any of these rough ideas may contain the seed of greatness, but they all need to be given a chance to survive the first meeting.

That is why collecting raw materials and developing ideas must be regarded as two entirely separate phases. In the first stage, you can play around quite freely with the rough ideas and extract all kinds of interesting possibilities from them. In the second, you place each of these fragments under the microscope, weighing up the pros and cons until gradually you build the foundations of workable solutions. The aim is to fish out as many raw ideas as possible from the pool, and then to flesh them out to see if they will stand up to an initial critical analysis. In my experience, the first round of talks hardly ever produces a significant number of original and workable ideas. Of course there is the occasional exception, but nine times out of ten the project requires a lot more cogitation, experimentation and perspiration before ideas are ready to be put into practice.

In the fields of advertising, marketing, packaging design, events planning and new media, the second phase of ideas development plays a crucial role, because it is assumed that most of the approaches inherent in the pool of materials have already been used, and so any original idea needs to be thoroughly examined from every angle to see if it can be made into a functioning reality. During this process, do not underestimate the power of words. Those first creative meetings should not be called 'brainstorming'. That way you will avoid the pressure of high expectations.

It's far more accurate to talk about collecting raw materials: using a mixture of curiosity, fun and creativity, you should be hunting for rough nuggets of ideas, not the finished articles.

▼ Strategy: In its new store in Paris, Adidas presents the state-of-the-art image of a brand that makes full use of innovative technology and the latest scientific research to provide the best possible service to its customers. For instance, an LED catwalk offers a new form of technology that scans the foot, using infrared to pass the data to a computer interface that figures out the exact shape of shoe required. The design of this in-store concept combines complex aspects of media technology, functionality and ergonomics to create a futuristic shopping experience.

Client adidas AG | Agency Mutabor Design

Talking point: Imagine presenting this project to a creative meeting in a single sentence. How would you have assessed what would then have been the mere germ of an idea for an 'Innovation Centre'? Basic concepts like this will only get a fair chance if initially they are seen as neutral material to be developed until they can be subjected to – and can withstand – criticism from both inside and outside the creative team.

◀ **Strategy:** The luggage conveyor belts at Venice's Marco Polo airport are designed to look like a roulette wheel. Passengers collecting their luggage are offered free entry to the Casinò di Venezia for one night.

Talking point: If you present an idea like this to your colleagues, using only a few words, everyone will immediately be enthusiastic. But there will be at least half a dozen other ideas that need to be developed first, before the team can fully appreciate their originality and potential. That is why every starting point that emerges from the first creative meeting needs to be regarded as raw material and not as a fully fledged idea. Only then can exotic, eccentric and outlandish ideas escape being prematurely evaluated and rejected as unrealistic.

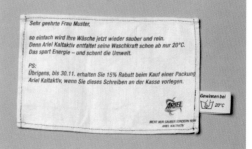

▲ **Strategy:** Ariel Coldactive gets washing clean at 20° C. To show its power, the company sent out a direct mail containing a piece of black fabric and a sample of the detergent. When the fabric is washed with Ariel, it turns into a piece of white fabric that is also a money-off coupon.

USE SEARCH FIELDS TO BOOST CREATIVITY

When creatives sit biting their fingernails in despair, it's often because expectations are too high or goals are unclear. But mostly it's because they're simply lacking in inspiration.

Supposing you're looking for ideas to promote an event based on the theme of extreme sports. It might be helpful, even before you start collecting raw materials, to prepare 'search fields' to boost creativity. Search fields are subjects that have nothing to do with the actual content of the project, but may nevertheless provide impulses for exciting new ideas. In this instance, we might consider images of the ten biggest construction sites in the world, and our question would be: how could we use the image of a dam, a tunnel or a skyscraper under construction to promote a new sport? Another fruitful search field might be images of thirty of the most unusual landscapes on Earth. What could sportsmen and women do in these places that no one has ever dared to do before? What new sports or equipment might these landscapes inspire? You could use photographs, films, articles, drawings, maps or even sound files as a jumping-off point. The aim is to get your team to make unusual connections by confronting them with apparently irrelevant information.

These images are always at their most effective when the creatives themselves have absolutely no idea what, say, the wild landscape of Cappadocia in Turkey actually looks like. This involves knowledge that they either do not have or would not normally connect with the task in hand. Another search field for extreme sports might be a compilation of the twenty crazy situations or action scenes from different computer games. Using a starting point like this, teams of four could be given, say, fifty minutes during the first raw materials phase to come up with as many ideas as possible relating to their project. Search fields are a great way to kick-start the creative process. The following points need to be borne in mind: you have to choose the fields very carefully beforehand, because not every subject will be suitable or inspirational. The key question is always what unrelated images seem most likely to set creative minds in motion, and for this reason, the material must be well researched and prepared. Don't give the team all your surprises at once – leave a gap between each search field. Teams need a little time to consider each one and immerse themselves in the subject. For a successful session of idea collecting on a theme like extreme sports, three or four search fields should be enough, using three teams of four to work on them. By the end, you should have between 100 and 200 rough ideas in the pool.

▶ **Strategy:** Touchgrind is a multitouch skateboard game for the iPhone, and it uses finger movements to steer the skateboard on spectacular journeys over ramps and obstacles or over open ground. An online level editor offers players the chance to create their own skateparks and share them with other people all over the world.

Client Illusion Labs AB | Creative Mirabelle Looft

Talking point: Make a short list of potential search fields that might help you to create brand new iPhone games. Go to a rehab centre, study the training programme for NASA astronauts, or delve into the world of a rock band. Any of these search fields could lead to dozens of ideas for new games.

▶ **Strategy:** The Coca-Cola interactive vending machine has been fitted with a large touchscreen to bring customers into closer contact with the brand: HD video sequences, motion graphics, games and Bluetooth downloads are all available.

Client Coca-Cola | Agency Sapient / Samsung

Talking point: What sort of search fields would offer the greatest potential for exploiting all the possibilities of the Coca-Cola interactive vending machine? Jukeboxes, robots and mobile phones are probably too obvious and would only lead to commonplace ideas. Instead, think of motor cars, a ski trip to the Alps, or a nurse.

MAKE 200 RAW IDEAS YOUR MINIMUM

Many people at creative meetings waste most of their time trying to find the quickest short cut to the big idea. All that effort disguises the simple fact that there are no short cuts.

If you want to create a relaxed atmosphere at a creative meeting, you should start off by accepting the fact that 95 per cent of all potential ideas that are generated will end up in the bin. But that's no tragedy, because in the long term all you need are one or two strokes of greatness that will actually be put into action. Once this fact is established, the way is clear for people to play around as freely as they like with their raw ideas. Anyone who complains that this is a waste of time is clearly under the illusion that they can cut out all the crazy, impractical schemes by plucking the perfect solution out of a hat. This is an absurd concept of creativity, which inevitably leads most of its proponents into mediocrity. The results of taking short cuts like this are nearly always the same: second-hand ideas with slight modifications. The exciting thing about idea development is that you start off not knowing where or when you might suddenly find a pearl. For this reason, it's clear that the more material you generate, the greater the chances of finding a gem. I call this the lotto principle. With every extra entry you make, you increase your chances of hitting the jackpot. For instance, if you want to find an original way of promoting the extra sharp tang of a new brand of ketchup, you'll probably need more than 200 different starting points in order to come up with one truly original idea with the wow factor. It's relatively rare that people strike gold; sometimes they make do with silver, and many campaigns go down like lead. There is another important reason for developing a large number of ideas: creatives who produce only two or three tend to defend their 'babies' with tooth and claw, even if everyone else can see that they're worthless. But if you come up with 200 or more, no one will bat an eyelid if a lot of them fail to make it through to the next round. Everyone's attitude will be more relaxed and less emotional, which of course makes it far easier to judge ideas objectively.

Talking point: If you have a lot of people thinking for long enough about the same subject, almost inevitably there will be a lot of similar ideas. That's why I don't think that the ideas underlying these three campaigns were consciously copied. It's more likely that the creatives were under so much time pressure that their chains of association led them all to the most obvious image. Do your creative teams know how much time they need to develop their raw materials into ideas? Time is the decisive factor if you're going to delve deep into a subject and come up with something entirely new.

► **Strategy:** The labels on these two bottles of wine are based on pages from a wall calendar.

Client **Weingut M. Machalek** | Creative **Max Jurasch**

Talking point: There is nothing more relaxing than a bubbling stream of ideas. Interestingly, in a long session it's often towards the end that the best ideas emerge, because the pressure eases and everybody is in a lighter mood.

217

▼ **Strategy:** This CD cover for the band Concave Scream can be used as a calendar. A dial in the cover can be turned to the month, and if the CD is positioned in the right place, it shows the day.

Client **Concave Scream** | Agency **Kinetic Singapore**

Talking point: The more raw material for ideas you develop, the faster you can jettison the clichés. Get two teams to compete against each other. The winner will be the one that comes up with the largest number of crazy ideas. The result will be useful for two reasons: firstly, you will now have a large pool of suggestions, and secondly you will have raw material that is likely to produce amazing solutions like the one above, rather than the usual humdrum offerings.

▶ **Strategy:** This print campaign for K-fee shows the explosive effects when milk meets caffeine.

Client **K-fee** | Agency **Jung von Matt**

Milk meets caffeine

Talking point: Can you name the three biggest obstacles that would prevent your team from developing more than 100 rough ideas in two hours?

Ideas come from the head, but it's only when they are described, written down or sketched that they are truly born.

Jotting down a few rudimentary ideas is usually much simpler than suddenly finding yourself having to record 200 or more of them in one sitting. In the latter instance, one unfortunate team member will be condemned to spend the whole meeting writing or sketching. Thoughts are fleeting, and ideas come and go as quickly as you can say 'Eureka!', so this is a problem that needs careful attention. The following five tips will increase the chances of survival for your newborn 'babies':

▶ Describe an idea in two sentences.
▶ Write down an idea in three sentences.
▶ Sketch an idea with a few strokes of the pen.
▶ Draw an idea as a plan or map.
▶ Make an idea tangible in the form of a dummy or prototype.

When a team of four is working efficiently, they will produce a regular flow of rough ideas which can best be recorded on pre-prepared 'idea sheets'. One sheet per idea will be enough to take you through to the next phase. Ideally, these ideas should be noted down by the person responsible for choosing the team for that particular project. The raw material can then be taken away for further processing or evaluation, and can be worked on by other teams. The idea sheet should contain a space for sketches, should include the title of the meeting, and should allow ideas to be sorted into three categories: 'usable', 'needs work', 'unusable'. These sheets also offer another interesting way of extracting more possibilities from unused fragments: make an ideas jigsaw. You take the separate, fragmentary ideas out of the pool, and put them together in different combinations. This can often lead to a second creative phase that produces surprising results. However, anyone who works alone instead of with a team, and is charged with the task of finding solutions in all situations, should always have some means of recording these fleeting moments of inspiration – on a PDA, a laptop, or a good old-fashioned notebook. Even if the thoughts come in a haphazard fashion at first, eventually connections may become more apparent, and can lead to a more complete image. Thomas Edison and Leonardo da Vinci worked in just this manner, and later extracted some of their greatest work from their notebooks.

This trade stand for PROJEKTPILOT was made from 8,140 cardboard tubes, measuring over 10 km (6 miles) in total length and weighing almost 18 tonnes, stuck together to form a huge, organically curved structure.

Client PROJEKTPILOT
Agency D'art Design Gruppe

Talking point: At a creative meeting, how would you record this idea to increase its chances of survival? In a sentence, in a sketch, or as a paper model?

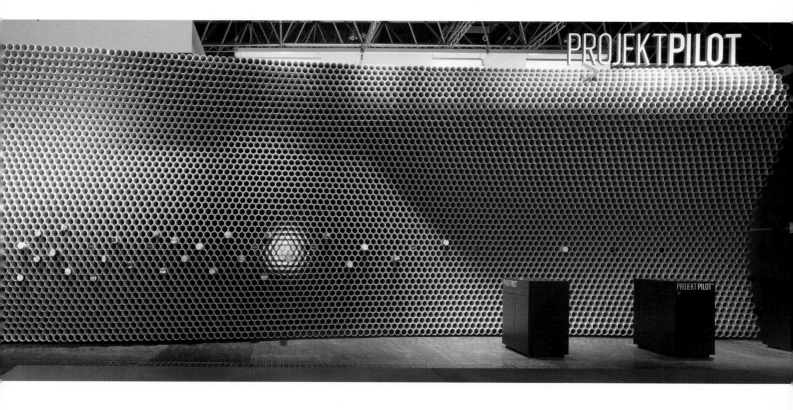

Credits Autodesk/
The Grove Consultants International

▲ **Strategy:** Multitouch technology offers a wonderful way of combining, developing and presenting ideas, sketches and rudimentary concepts. Team members can send their designs in advance to the conference room, so that they're ready and waiting to be worked on by all concerned.

Talking point: What new ways of recording and processing ideas would be useful to your team in future?

All the information in the world counts for little if it is not continually being linked together in useful and surprising ways. By the same token, creativity is of little use if there is not enough relevant information available to link the two together in new patterns at the right moment to form meaningful innovations.

Whether you're in search of new ideas for events, product designs, TV formats, online games or campaigns, stage shows or product presentations, you need to gauge just when, where and how information should be supplied. In the three creative phases described below, it is particularly important to know when you should present the team with certain facts, and when you should withhold them. For instance, during the raw materials phase, it's useful to make available lots of information about products, facts or situations, but all the related rules, laws, habits, expectations, emotions, assumptions and rituals are best left in the background.

This will be clearer if we look at an example. Let's assume that you and your team are alien visitors who have just landed on Planet Earth. You're taken into a room containing three objects which you have never seen before and which you don't know the first thing about. It is this kind of situation that gives you the

greatest amount of creative freedom, because you are not encumbered with any foreknowledge. The three objects present you with a certain number of options – you can have a casual look at them, or you can take them apart and put them back together again in a new and perhaps useful combination. With every object presented to the team, the number of possible combinations increases, as does the chance of innovations. If you filled the room with hundreds of objects, you would get a playing field of almost infinite possibilities. However, the moment you tell your team that they are not allowed to change the appearance of any red objects, you will have introduced a rule that immediately reduces the number of possible variations. The more of these rules you introduce into the game, the more rapidly the range of options will narrow down. What effect do you think the following rules would have on your team's creativity? Until now, round objects have always been used only by women, and this must remain so for the future. Objects that are heavier than air can't fly, and so flying is forbidden. Hollow objects are worthless, according to a centuries-old tradition. In short, it can be said that the more unfamiliar and stimulating information you can present to your team, the more possibilities for original ideas they will produce. But the more rules you confront them with, in the form of foreknowledge, traditions, customs, experiences, assumptions, cultural taboos, habits and laws, the narrower the playing field will become.

The most dangerous of all the rules and regulations are those that people are not consciously aware of. Creatives can be left dangling like puppets on their strings but still believing they have creative freedom. But if you are armed with this knowledge, you will be able to give your team effective guidance. Your aim should be to spark off a creative revolution by introducing new and unusual information, while at the same time reducing the number of participants by excluding those who always want to apply their own specialist experience and standards. However, if your aim is the evolutionary development of existing ideas, you had better reduce the unfamiliar information and increase the proportion of old hands at this particular game. Another example of how information can steer the thoughts of your team members is the following: in order to produce greater creative freedom during the raw materials phase, withhold certain information. You might give your team the task of generating as many raw ideas as possible in answer to the question: How can you keep the attention of children? Your team is allowed to do whatever it likes. But to begin with, you don't tell them the concrete problem you are trying to solve. Only when they have come up with a large selection of rough ideas do you give them another piece of information about the true goal, in order to help them in the developmental

phase: How might a website motivate children to take part in a competition? Now the team can look back over the collected fragments, and put some of the relevant ones together to create the first concepts to be developed. It is essential, however, that for the first step they should not be given information that would restrict their field of thought or would lead them to recall any knowledge or experiences they might already have had.

Collecting raw materials

For this phase, try inviting to the meeting as many people as possible who have no experience of your field and don't know any of the rules and regulations that govern it. Their 'naivety' will give them maximum creative latitude, and will compel your 'specialists' to come out of their conventional shells. Another way of extending creative openness is to make your team members aware of all the professional and cultural standards, traditions, rules of conduct and common experiences in your field by writing them down. Then everyone should set about breaking them, transcending them, or replacing them. However, what is even more important during this phase is to feed the team with unfamiliar information from different fields, as well as surprising details about the subject itself, going way beyond the range of general knowledge. Leave the doors and windows wide open, and let in the fresh air. You'll be surprised how many cobwebs get blown away.

Idea development

After 50 to 70 minutes of collecting raw ideas, the team will enter the next phase with a pool containing hundreds of rough nuggets. Each of these should now be twisted and turned, tried and tested until it's clear whether or not it has enough potential to be developed further. During this process, the team must reconcile two opposites: on the one side, they must use their specialist skills and knowledge to push the rough idea towards implementation, and on the other they must apply their creativity to see whether the problems they discover can actually lead to some dazzlingly brilliant solution. This is the seemingly impossible task that faces every creative team: to create a synthesis of information and imagination that really works.

Idea evaluation

This phase definitely requires specialist information – the more, the better. In addition, however, creatives must be able to think in terms of solutions and not just problems. If, for example, they discover a small obstacle within an otherwise brilliant idea, it will be the team's overall mindset that decides whether the idea is scrapped or given further thought. Attitudes should always be kept positive.

◀ **Strategy:** WiiSpray has been developed for the Nintendo Wii remote, and it works just like a real can of spraypaint but it's entirely virtual. You can easily change caps and colours and it's totally intuitive to use. The art that you produce with it can be saved and digitally edited.

Talking point: What information was needed for the development of this idea? What existing ideas were transformed into something new through the changing of certain rules? Don't skate over the surface of this idea, but try to delve down into its depths.

edex.com   0800 703 3339

▲ Strategy:
FedEx Express.

Talking point: What information was needed for this idea? What information should be withheld from the team during the collection of materials, in order not to inhibit creativity?

Knowledge is the raw material that creatives use to make their ideas. Creating ideas out of nothing is God's prerogative!

Suppose you have been commissioned to design a new, breathable sports shoe and incorporate it into a screenplay for a thriller, or portray its benefit in an ad campaign. No matter which of these tasks you're working on, the question is what knowledge you actually have on the subject of shoes and feet. Most creatives would probably dip into their everyday experiences – whatever they've heard, read or seen for themselves. But if you're to come up with something really original, a decisive factor might well be some specialist information. How many bones there are in a foot? How often does a foot shed its skin? How many litres of sweat does a foot produce in a year? What is the difference between a woman's sweat and a man's? How many years does it take for a bone to become deformed by regular pressure? Do toes have distinctive prints, like fingers? What kinds of bacteria live inside shoes? Why do some pets hide their owner's shoes, or like to sleep on them? There are lots and lots of weird facts and figures such as these that can provide a spur for original ideas. The quality of these ideas will always depend on the raw material from which they are fashioned. What about the shoe itself? What do you know about new fabrics, of which there are hundreds every year? What do you know about new trends in architecture, fashion design, or product design? What do you know? In other words, how do you expect to come up with a brilliantly original idea for a sports shoe if all you can do is draw on knowledge available to everybody else in the field?

It is said that knowledge doubles every five years. Two centuries ago there were still plenty of polymaths around, but today, fields like materials technology, architecture, design, film, fashion and advertising are mostly full of specialists who know more and more about less and less. Of course the professionals in the creative industries have their own skills to offer, but every day they also need to acquire relevant knowledge about the subjects they have to tackle. And so once again I'd like to return to the knowledge broker or infomediary, whose vital role I have already mentioned in Chapter 3. Knowledge brokers are not a luxury but a necessity. Particularly during the raw materials phase, they can work miracles for your team by regularly providing the information you need. The selection and preparation of this material will be a decisive factor in the quality and quantity of ideas that your team will come up with. This is not just a matter of depth (highly specialized knowledge) but also of breadth (taking in a variety of fields). Here's how to get the fountain of knowledge bubbling:

- ▶ Make knowledge brokers a permanent fixture in your team.
- ▶ Invite specialists from other fields.
- ▶ Set up databases .
- ▶ Build up your own in-house library.
- ▶ Cooperate with companies in different fields.
- ▶ Incorporate the client's own knowledge.
- ▶ Use market and opinion research.
- ▶ Engage external advisers.

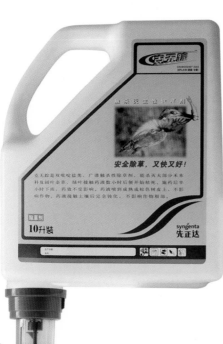

◀ **Strategy:** Syngenta were commissioned to design a new crop-protection dispenser to be used by hundreds of thousands of smallholders in China and India. Their solution was the PortA Pac system, with individual components that can be reused and refilled. Insecticides can be dispensed securely, storage is made easy and wastage and packaging is minimized.

Client Syngenta Corp Protection | Agency pi global

Talking point: If a knowledge broker were a permanent member of your team, supplying them with stimulating material and current information, how could this help to provide innovative solutions to complex problems like the above?

▼ **Strategy:** This 'Flower Lamp' shines brightest when electricity consumption is at its lowest in the house. It rewards the occupants by automatically opening its 'petals', but as consumption rises, they close up again.

Credits Front/Interactive Institute

Talking point: In the hands of creative teams, knowledge can become magical raw material. If you share it with others, you won't lose it – you will double it. And if you're inventive enough to combine wildly diverse sources of information, you can create new values, uses and meanings.

Generally it's not an idea itself that leads to failure, but the way we think about it. When our minds are focused on the negative, we are unable to see many potential solutions.

Imagine that you and two colleagues are in the raw materials phase, trying to come up with as many rough ideas as possible. Then you realize that your colleagues are finding it hard to take your suggestions and run with them. Instead, they offer nothing but objections, saying that this proposal is weak and that one can't possibly work. What is missing here is positive thinking. This is the most vital factor if ideas are to be given a fair chance of being implemented. Positive thinking is not just a special creative technique – it can be applied in all areas of life. In a creative context, however, it can be divided into three categories:

Opportunities

You may well spot a problem that may make an idea unworkable right at the start. Instead of scrapping it, however, give it a chance by asking the following question: if this idea won't work for one reason or another, what new opportunities might this problem open up? Instead of criticizing, feed your answers back to the team to spark off new approaches.

Alternatives

Again, let's start by imagining a problem that might get an idea disqualified from consideration. Try to rescue it by asking what changes need to be made in order to solve the problem. If, for instance, the issue is that something is too small or too expensive, see if you can make the whole thing bigger or cheaper. Don't just confine yourself to a single solution, but find as many as possible in order to maximize the chances of saving the idea. Again, instead of criticism, feed the answers back to your colleagues as alternative solutions.

New possibilities

Once again imagine that the starting point is a problem, and once again, rather than scrap the idea, try asking a a question: does this seedling possess the potential to grow into a truly original idea? You can rescue it by getting it to sprout into something new. In this case, you will feed new ideas back to your team instead of criticism.

Thinking positive requires practice, but in my view it is one of the key tools for anyone whose job is to develop and implement ideas. It's worth noting that many highly gifted creatives practise this approach quite automatically, and time and again it enables them to turn even the most radical and impossible projects into flourishing successes. However, the majority of people tend intuitively to focus on difficulties and to deal with them in the swiftest manner possible – namely, by jettisoning the idea. This can result in the loss of some hugely promising ideas and the survival of others that are merely mediocre. Positive, opportunistic thinking is essential to the creative process, and without it, the creative blockage can be so serious that the entire process can grind to a halt. You need the ability to spot alternative approaches and new pathways instead of conventional routes and old obstacles, and this need becomes urgent if originality is the ultimate goal. The fresh seeds will be allowed to grow, and will be all the stronger when they come to be tested for workability in the next phase. Albert Einstein once said: 'You can recognize a really good idea by the fact that seems impossible to implement in the first place.' The more radical and alien it seems, the more susceptible it will be to harsh criticism, and that is why it needs the solid support of positive thinking. Of course that doesn't mean that you should shut your eyes to problems. On the contrary, during the raw materials phase, these can be discussed quite openly, but the discussion should always be approached in terms of problem-solving – remember you're helping the idea and rescuing it, not hindering and killing it.

Client **Expedia.com** | Agency **Serviceplan/Mediaplus**

▶ **Strategy:** The travel website Expedia wanted to advertise on TV, but couldn't afford an expensive campaign. Their solution was a live 'guerrilla' campaign on several weather channels. Making use of the cold winter weather, they sent out small teams to stand in front of the fixed cameras and hold up large banners marked with special summer offers and their web address. The images were beamed out directly by the weather stations.

Talking point: What kind of approach could you take to this idea that would ensure that you could find plenty of potential solutions to any problems that arose? And what kind of approach would allow you to find lots of apparently insoluble problems, in order to strangle the idea at birth? Positive thinking is a matter of developing an attitude that will lead you to see everything as an opportunity.

▼ **Strategy:** Up to 40,000 spectators line an artificial ice track to watch a Red Bull Crashed Ice event. Four skaters compete against one another wearing full ice hockey kit and racing along a 400-metre downhill track with chicanes, jumps and curves. These events have already brought action and drama to Lausanne, Stockholm, Moscow, Prague and the US.

Talking point: The quest for originality and higher standards is fuelled by positive thinking and never being satisfied with what you have. Have a look at some established ideas in fields like events, packaging, product design and marketing, and see how you might reinvent them. Search for opportunities, and develop as many variations as possible so that you're making these ideas more exciting and unusual, and taking them to the next level.

Got an idea that doesn't work? Congratulations, you've just found a problem! Now can you imagine developing a solution for this problem, or would you rather ignore the problem and throw it away, along with the idea?

After collecting raw materials, your team should have a large pool of rudimentary ideas. If you find you've got a lot of crazy, totally unrealistic bits and pieces in the pool, that's a good sign that you're on to something special. If the response is heated discussion, astonishment, disbelief or other such extremes, you are definitely on the right track. The stronger the reactions, the more sure you can be that these ideas are genuinely original.

At the same time, your team should realize that these ideas need very careful handling during the next phase of development. The majority will probably be impractical and won't stand up to critical analysis, and that's why the team needs the ability to seek out and openly discuss problems while at the same time reversing their critical approach so that instead they focus on solutions. It may sound a little schizophrenic, but every team member needs to be a realist and a fantasist at the same time. For a solution-seeker, an 'idea-killer' is worth its weight in gold, because it can help to turn a weakness into a strength. But a person who can only see the negative side will systematically block every fresh approach. That is where the positive thinking discussed in the previous section comes into play, because it can function like a mini creative meeting, providing good ideas for rescuing bad ideas.

Let's say your clients have a problem: visitors to their trade stand are wary of getting too close to their products and are too timid to test them. A simple goal formulation would be: how can we encourage visitors to make closer contact with the product? During the raw materials phase, you and your team compile the usual pool of rough ideas, and in the next phase you examine them to see which of them are worth developing. When you work on the first one, you come up against a problem: then either you discard the idea or you develop an idea to solve the problem. Some 90 per cent of people will choose the former course, and will thus break off the creative process. It's therefore stuck halfway, and can never be completed. As we have seen, the outcome can only be mediocre or overused ideas.

If you have people like that in your team, get rid of them. What good can they possibly be doing? People who think solely in terms of problems without solutions are not creatives.

▼ **Strategy:** Wearing specially developed Red Bull carbon-fibre wings, BASE jumper Felix Baumgartner succeeded in flying the 36 km (22 miles) between Dover and Calais. At a height of 9,800 metres (32,000 ft), he jumped out of a transport plane and without any artificial means of propulsion, reaching a maximum speed of 360 kph (225 mph), headed for France. After six minutes and 22 seconds, he opened his parachute and landed on the French coast.

Talking point: In the quest for functional carbon-fibre wings, hundreds of ideas must have emerged that showed why it couldn't be done. Each problem presented a challenge to the team to find a creative solution. Thinking positively means looking for solutions until you finally achieve your goal.

Client Natural Crisps Limited | Agency Ziggurat Brand Consultants

▼ **Strategy:** These Jonathan Crisp potato chip packets make fun of the British upper classes, but one of them looked so much like Princess Anne that the company had to change the design, following complaints by the Royal Family!

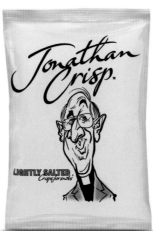

Talking point: If you want an unusual idea to survive the raw materials phase, you had better consolidate it as quickly as possible. Look for and discuss any weaknesses, but make sure that you finish the criticism by adding: how can we solve these problems? Think positively – it's an ability that can be learned as easily as watching TV.

CRITICISM IS GOOD, BUT MAKE IT CONCRETE

The head of marketing looks at the design for a banner campaign and says, 'It's pretty good, but could it look a little less cheerful?' The designer replies, 'Should we add some more red?' The head of marketing says, 'No, better not – that looks even more cheerful!'

So how cheerful does he want it to be? Could it be that he doesn't actually have a clue? That's what often happens when people come up with criticisms along the lines of 'It doesn't feel right.' If they can't justify their comments, they should think before they speak. Only if a criticism is articulated clearly and precisely can the person on the receiving end regard it as constructive and as a possible challenge. So for potential critics, the rule is to make the criticisms concrete. Otherwise, the positive thinking process will break down completely. Without a clear problem, you can't expect a clear solution. Vague comments like 'It doesn't look like our style' should be avoided at all costs. This raises the following questions: What exactly IS your style? What exactly are you afraid we might come up with? What exactly are you afraid might be the consequences of what you are afraid we might come up with? Who exactly would be affected by the consequences of what you are afraid we might come up with? What exactly are the negative feelings that might be aroused in them? Is your fear based on

instinct or on provable facts? Now perhaps you understand what I mean by 'concrete' criticism. 'It isn't our style' doesn't give anybody a chance to rescue an idea or to find a solution. It's totally negative and totally destructive. Breaking this rule can have a devastating effect – it's almost like sending a child out into the street without first explaining how to cross the road safely. And yet the rule is broken every hour of every day in creative agencies all round the world. It applies, of course, just as much to the client as to the agency. Here are a few more dreaded comments:

- ► I'm just not feeling it.
- ► It's kind of boring.
- ► Can't we do better than that?
- ► It'll never work.
- ► People are just going to laugh at us.
- ► Would it look better in a different colour?
- ► Surely this has all been done before?
- ► Non-verbal criticism: raised eyebrows, loud sighs, rolling the eyes.

▼ **Strategy:** This design for Urban Decay lip gloss by HCT Packaging is lip-smacking for two reasons: firstly, it has the delicious taste of crème brulée, and secondly, the cap contains a pin-up boy whose clothes come off when you turn the cap 180 degrees.

Client **Urban Decay** | Design **HCT Packaging/Urban Decay**

Talking point: 'The design's too much like other make-up brands, and the pin-up boys are so cheesy that there's no way our target group would go for it!' Vague criticism like this offers no room for a solution to rescue the idea. Is there anyone in your team who can make sure that the basic rules of criticism are adhered to?

THE JIGSAW TECHNIQUE

Teams invest a great deal of energy in building up big collections of raw ideas, but then they stop halfway. The jigsaw technique is the simplest trick I know to get one and one to make three.

The jigsaw technique is a vital intermediate stage on the way to a great idea. Inexplicably, most creatives in meetings tend to look at the individual ideas that emerge from the mass of raw materials one by one. If only they looked more carefully at the whole collection, they might discover parallels and overlaps between the pieces, which could lead to completely new ideas. It therefore makes sense to spend a little time putting the pieces together in whatever fancy ways you please, to see if a bigger picture emerges. Think of the technique as a kaleidoscope that allows you to shake things around to make different patterns. Let yourself be surprised by what you find. It's worth spending 30 to 40 minutes making idea jigsaws, just as long as each player keeps a positive, creative attitude, focusing on possibilities and opportunities rather than problems. The latter will only come into play once the game is over.

Credits Talpa Content B.V.

◄ Strategy: *Dating in the Dark* is a reality dating show in which three single men and three single women are put in a house together but are kept strictly separate. The only way they can get to know one another is by meeting in a room that's kept in total darkness. After a few days, the contestants choose the partner they would most like to meet in daylight. Afterwards, they get to decide whether they want to meet again or go their separate ways.

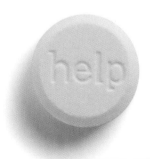

▶ Strategy: Help Remedies were developed to offer straightforward treatments for simple health problems.

Complicated packaging and instructions have been replaced by clarity, simplicity and plenty of clean white space.

help
I've cut myself™

8 clear bandages. Two sizes

Hello. I'm sorry you cut yourself. It could be an isolated incident, or maybe you are a very clumsy person. Don't worry. The clumsy are much more lovable than the graceful. The graceful are always busy ballet dancing, and doing incredible feats on the trapeze. The clumsy are always busy being coddled, rubbed, and cared for.

So if you're not too busy having attractive persons ravish you with affection, take a minute to care for your injury. Wash it, and lay one of our pretty bandages on top. In a matter of moments you will be able to return to your clumsy affairs.

Talking point: Take one of these two ideas and split it up into individual elements to see how the components fit together. Then take each component and find as many ways as possible to improve it. When you've come up with 30 or more improvements, start combining the elements of the original idea with the new ones until you come up with a different but workable concept. This is how you can use the jigsaw technique to improve existing concepts or push them in different directions.

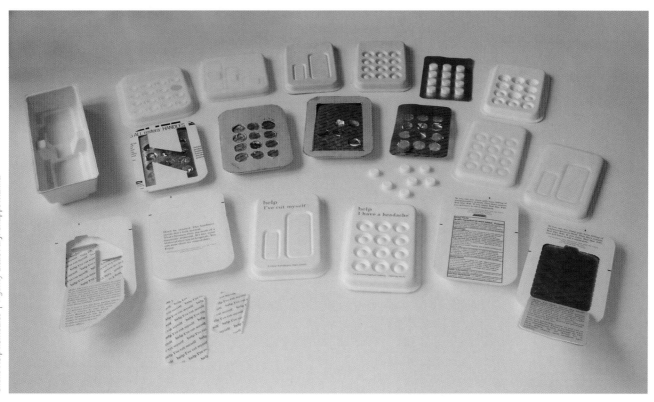

Client Help Remedies | Agency Little Fury/Chapps Malina

EVERY IDEA HAS AN UNDERLYING PATTERN

Great ideas are exciting and surprising. However, the basic motif or pattern behind them, which is what arouses these reactions, tends to remain hidden from most people. Others not only see the pattern but also see endless variations that might be developed from it.

Identifying and understanding the pattern behind an idea gives you almost unlimited freedom to vary and change it. In combination with positive thinking, this is an invaluable talent if creative teams want to work their way towards original ideas. Anyone who is happy to switch off after the very first variation has probably missed their chance to find something really great. In my previous books, *Creative Advertising* and *Visual Creativity*, I examined these patterns in detail, and showed how they could be used to develop completely new and original ideas. If you study the campaigns that have won awards at international advertising festivals, you will soon see that the vast majority are based on 40 to 50 patterns that recur again and again. These are rather like containers that can be filled with all sorts of liquids. Theoretically, there seems little chance of direct repetition, since the number of fillings and combinations is virtually infinite. In other words, this is not a matter of copying or stealing ideas, but of understanding how to use these basic patterns in order to create ideas of your own. The following are just a selection from the 50 or so patterns that I listed in my earlier books:

▶ mixing and matching
▶ compare and contrast
▶ exaggeration
▶ turning things around
▶ omission and suggestion
▶ playing with time
▶ a change of perspective
▶ double meanings
▶ metaphor and analogy
▶ breaking out the frame
▶ alter the product
▶ changing the surface
▶ taking a look inside

If you want to train your own creativity and learn to recognize these patterns, try taking a look at the work of prizewinners at international festivals, and then test yourself in two ways: first, give a precise but concise summary of the goal behind the work; secondly, describe the pattern underlying the work in a single sentence, and then transform it into as many variations as possible, or use it as your starting point for completely new ideas.

Credits From a campaign for Mercedes-Benz | Illustrator Max Julian Otto

The new S-Class is coming.

Mercedes-Benz

◄ Strategy: 'The new S-Class is coming. Mercedes-Benz.'

Talking point: To work out the pattern here, first ask yourself what might have been the goal formulation that the team worked with. How can you show in a campaign that the new S-Class is going to be the top car in its range? Next you should try to imagine how the team would have approached the goal. Did they think in terms of exaggeration, contrasts, metaphors? The actual pattern might be summarized as follows: this product (car) is so precious that its location (garage) ought to be turned into a palace. Once you have analysed the pattern, you can use its different components to develop your own variations: apart from a crystal chandelier, what else could you put in the garage to make it a suitable home for a luxury product? Oil paintings, air conditioning, a flatscreen TV? What settings could you use to indicate through exaggeration that this product is particularly valuable? A motorway, a car dealership, a carwash, a driveway? How would the superiority of the product be viewed by competitors, neighbours, other drivers? Look at the subject from different perspectives. What effects does the product benefit have on you even before you buy it? What might be the sales or delivery process for such a luxurious car?

◀ **Strategy:** People who sit down at this bus stop in Rotterdam are automatically weighed, and their weight flashes up on a screen. A service provided by the fitness chain Fitness First.

Talking point: Play around with patterns in order to create your own variations. These will provide a faster route to good solutions than getting stuck with your very first idea. What do you think is the pattern behind the ideas shown here?

▶ **Strategy:** The viral ad 'Extreme LED Sheep Art' shows shepherds and sheepdogs herding a flock of sheep to create huge animated images: a giant sheep, a firework display, the computer game Pong, or the Mona Lisa. Some scenes make use of LED lights by Samsung, who commissioned the film.

◀ **Strategy:** The pages of this calendar are designed to resemble an overgrown lawn. But with every page that you remove, the 'grass' looks a little neater, and by the end of the year, it is beautifully trimmed. The last page shows the lawnmower, which can perform the task with ease and efficiency.

Talking point: How would you describe the pattern behind this idea? How could you transform a public space into a screen on which freely moving elements could be manipulated in such a way that they form a picture? If you want to play around with this pattern, think of as many alternatives as possible to the key elements of field, sheep and shepherds, and develop new variations of your own.

Client **IKEA** | *Agency* **IKEA Design**

▲ **Strategy:** To mark the opening of a new IKEA store in Japan, the Kobe Portliner monorail was turned into a mobile showroom.

Talking point: People who think they've already found the perfect solution have probably overlooked the countless possible variations contained within that solution. How can you ensure that it becomes part of your team's standard procedure to seek out the pattern behind each idea and to work out additional variations in their quest for the best? This will ensure that only the most brilliantly original ideas are allowed to leave your agency!

THE PRELIMINARY PRESENTATION

If clients insist on being creative, this is their best opportunity. The challenge consists in developing workable solutions to overcome any weaknesses or failings in the ideas presented. But this should not be a forum for clients to promote their favourite colours or other matters of personal taste.

What objections can there be to involving the client in the creative process? None, provided that the team has the ability to initiate and steer that process. The key here is a clear allocation of roles and a professional style of presentation, which can turn creative chaos into productive order. There needs to be a careful and harmonious balance between the different interests of the client and the creatives. A special preliminary presentation therefore has the clear goal of showing clients the initial concepts, sketches or dummies with a view to their cooperation on further development. Under no circumstances should there be just one or two fully developed ideas, unlike most presentations, which virtually confront clients with a fait accompli. In those cases, clients have no choice other than to adopt the passive role of a critic whose sole right is to say yes or no. The role of the client here is to help test the practicality of some of the most promising concepts and solutions that have emerged from the pool, and to work side by side with the creatives in optimizing them. In this way, the client has

the chance to be involved early in the creative process and to steer the best ideas in the right direction.

The preliminary presentation is therefore a kind of creative coming together of the client and the agency, although it is the creatives who must decide the degree and manner in which the clients are to be involved. Their role is not to push through their own personal choice of colours, or to suddenly mutate into part-time designers, but to root out possible weaknesses in the concept and then to help to resolve them. The great advantage of this approach lies in the fact that the ideas of the creatives then automatically become the ideas of the client, so that the responsibility for their implementation is shared. It also removes any element of shock from the final presentation, because the client has been part of the evolutionary process. It is also extremely helpful to have support from someone high up in the client company when it comes to the final presentation – another short cut to success. It's all too often the case that creative teams have to go right back to square one after the final presentation, because the goal had never been made clear, and the clients sit there open-mouthed, confronted by ideas that are simply miles away from what they wanted. Many clients actually expect ideas they are already familiar with, so it's simpler to stick to the tried and trusted, but if you want to change direction, get the client involved as early as you can. The fact that this kind of preliminary presentation can also strengthen the relationship between client and agency goes without saying.

◄ **Strategy:** The staging for the MTV Video Music Awards in New York was designed by Mark Fisher around the theme of 'Pictures at an Exhibition'. The frames held video screens which were incorporated into the show, and the stage changed constantly with each phase of the ceremony.

Client MTV | Agency Stufish – The Mark Fisher Studio

Talking point: Use the preliminary presentation for a challenging exchange of roles: imagine that the client is trying to sell the ideas developed by the creative team to the agency. The client's team must come up with solid arguments as to why these ideas offer the best possible solution. The agency's team, on the other hand, will point out all the problems.

▶ **Strategy:** For the music video 'Her Morning Elegance' by Oren Lavie, 3,225 still images were taken by a camera hung from the ceiling. Using digital stop-motion techniques, these pictures were turned into a film with a unique visual style.

Credits Oren Lavie

Talking point: If the agency itself is the client, it may happen that too much self-criticism will nip good ideas in the bud. It can therefore be useful to give a kind of preliminary presentation to outsiders, just to get some constructive feedback and counter any self-criticism.

▶ **Strategy:** Target's outdoor promotional film 'Art Connects' combines various styles of art to create a new message. The central idea involves bringing two graffiti artists from different continents together in the digital world in order to make three films. Target's red logo features prominently in all of them.

Talking point: Who needs to be involved in the preliminary presentation in order to ensure that the key players are familiar with every stage of the process and feel that they are playing an active role in it? Will this accelerate the development of an idea like the one shown above?

If you hesitate, you're putting off both success and failure. This seems like a dilemma but isn't one – hesitation will cost you dear in both cases.

The ultimate decision-maker is the market, i.e. what marketing people call the target group. No matter how thorough and well-intentioned your creative experts, pollsters, clients and evaluation procedures may be, there is no substitute for a real-life test out in the commercial jungle. An early sortie can pay large dividends. Take your rough ideas, prototypes, patterns and models straight to your target group to see if you're on the right track. If you waste time on in-house tests, endless discussions, or timid diversionary tactics, you will achieve one of two things – delayed failure, or delayed success. And both of these things cost money. If you have the courage to get rid of the truly impractical schemes straight away, you will be able to concentrate all the more swiftly on those ideas

that really are workable. Incidentally, mistakes are relatively cheap at this early stage. There is also nothing more instructive than feedback from the market itself. If you're really smart, you can even get the target group involved with the idea development phase. Exposing ideas to the market as early as possible can work wonders in fields like packaging, online campaigns, store design and product development. You can quickly find out just how far you can go with your daring innovations and experiments, because it will soon become clear what works and what doesn't. It all follows the principle of 'the survival of the fittest', and the more mutations and variations you try out, the better your chances of finding an idea that is able to adapt to its commercial environment.

◀ **Strategy:**
Women just can't stay away from the new Renault Clio. In this online game, the aim is to free the car from its clingy fans as fast as possible by using the mouse to pull them to the top of the screen. On each new level, the number of 'fans' increases.

Talking point: How can the target group be involved early on in the development of a game like this, so that their feedback can help to improve it?

▶ **Strategy:** To celebrate the 25th anniversary of the company, Replay asked Joseph Rossi to design this luxurious packaging for a very special pair of jeans.

Talking point: Test a number of variations on your target group, and prepare to be surprised when they make their choice. A small-scale test could involve displaying three different types of packaging in a few stores, and then seeing which one attracts the most customers. A practical test is a good way of immunizing an idea against damaging criticism.

Credits Emma Smart

◀ Strategy: This sandwich packaging has been designed to add a touch of fun to any lunch break. Pictures on the inside make it look like you're at a dinner table, at a picnic, or on a beach with a bucket and spade.

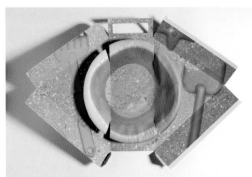

Talking point: Test your rudimentary ideas on the target group, and see how they react. You might be able to use their suggestions in surprising new ways. Always remember that they are the only real experts when it comes to judging whether your ideas are practical or not.

IDEA EVALUATION: KNOWING VERSUS FEELING

Almost all of us know of international successes that have come out of simple ideas. With hindsight, it seems perfectly obvious that they would become hits. Wouldn't it be wonderful if we already had this surefire instinct even when the ideas were regarded as crazy and unworkable by everybody else?

'Idea evaluation' sounds pretty straightforward to most people. It has a reassuring air, even though there's nothing reassuring about the process! In the creative industries, there are no clear parameters that can simply be applied in order to judge which ideas 'can't fail'. What makes a new trade stand, product, design, advertising campaign or TV show into a hit? Can you define the parameters before you actually start work? The desire to master the complexities of the world and the uncertainties of the future is so deeply ingrained in us that we are delighted to let ourselves be taken in by 'the ten commandments of marketing success', or 'eight secret paths to originality'. Unfortunately, real life doesn't work that way. Ideas are difficult to evaluate precisely because of the complex factors that decide whether something will click or not – our mental capacities just can't cope, at least on a conscious level. Some people are said to have a nose or a sixth sense for these things, though even they have been known to make mistakes. The 'gut feeling', however, is another crucial factor in deciding which ideas are ultimately to go out and seek your fortune. Of course the gut can also produce

nasty feelings of insecurity and downright fear, but if you haven't got the courage of your convictions, you might as well stay at home copying other people's ideas. Even star creatives whose instincts have already taken them to the loftiest heights don't actually have a patented formula, and have to start each project afresh with the same degree of risk. What distinguishes these people from the rest, however, is the self-confidence they have once they have made up their minds. This inner sense of security also earns the trust of their colleagues, clients and investors – a trust that would hardly be granted to those who radiate indecision. True innovators need the right mixture of knowledge, experience, intuition, and the self-assurance that this particular route is the one to follow. Quite apart from these basic qualities, there are of course certain criteria that can help us to evaluate ideas, and here are some of them:

The formulated goal

If the goal has been properly formulated at the start of the creative process, the chosen idea should provide the best possible answer to the question it asks. For example, what ideas or suggestions might motivate people playing a racing simulation game to swap information about their hobbies and interests? Your idea should provide a simple answer.

The brief and its parameters

This is the stage at which a good written brief comes into full effect. Ideally, it should contain important aids to evaluation, such as the budget, target group, brand values, and deadlines. If the brief is inadequate, it's best to sit down with the client before you start on the creative side of things, and compile a detailed list of parameters:

▶ Does this idea match our values and brand?
▶ Can it be completed within the given time?
▶ Is it really original?
▶ Is it unique and unmistakably ours?
▶ Is it within budget?
▶ Does it meet the needs of the target group?
▶ Does it fit with the aims of our long-term strategy?
▶ Is it easy to understand?
▶ Does it add value or possible uses?
▶ Does it engage the emotions?
▶ Is it workable?

Switching perspectives as a means of evaluation

There is no single, correct way to evaluate an idea, because its meaning and function depend to a huge extent on the perspective from which it is viewed. The simple but all-important question is which groups are being targeted and what needs are to be fulfilled. Teams can therefore judge ideas by looking at them through the eyes of different groups:

▶ How will this idea look from the perpective of the target group?
▶ How will it look from the client's perspective?
▶ What is its value in relation to the product?
▶ What is its value in relation to the competition?
▶ What does it mean from the perspective of the creative team?
▶ What impact will it have on the brand?

Checklist: ten ways to sabotage the evaluation

Here is a list of ten points that will guarantee a totally chaotic evaluation phase:

▶ Start the process without any evaluation criteria at all.
▶ During the evaluation process, be as subjective, unfair and sarcastic as possible.
▶ Defend no ideas except your own, no matter how mediocre they may be.
▶ Say you're happy with any old idea that comes up.
▶ Mock someone in front of the whole group.
▶ Give priority to ideas that already exist.
▶ Ignore your instincts and rely entirely on the checklist.
▶ Flog an idea to death until everyone agrees that it's no good.
▶ Focus on the negative.
▶ Drop unusual ideas as quickly as you can.

Client McDonald's/Coca-Cola | Agency DDB

Talking point: There are some ideas that are immediately appealing, but all the same no one can be sure whether the campaign will achieve its goal or merely impress the judges at some advertising festival.

Client Yiorgos Eleftheriades | Agency dARCHstudio

▲ **Strategy:** The interior of Yiorgos Eleftheriades's YEshop is made almost entirely of corrugated cardboard, which is both economical and 100 % recyclable. The flowing lines of the design are intended to create a multifunctional space that can be used as an exhibition hall, lounge area, party venue or space for fashion shows.

Talking point: Imagine you're only familiar with CDs and are being introduced to MP3s for the first time. What information or experiences would you need to judge how revolutionary the MP3 format will be? To a great extent, radical new ideas of this kind can't be tested against people's past experiences. As Henry Ford once remarked, 'If I had asked people what they wanted, they would have said faster horses.' What experiences would you call on to help you evaluate the YEshop?

'What, sir? You would make a ship sail against the wind and currents by lighting a bonfire under her decks? I pray you excuse me. I have no time to listen to such nonsense.'

Napoleon Bonaparte (1769–1821)

From today's perspective, Monsieur Bonaparte is making a fool of himself. But when he spoke those words, the French emperor was mocking a man who was proposing a new method of steam locomotion to modernize the French Navy. Even if you may find it hard to accept, you and I would probably have been among the 99 per cent of people who agreed with Napoleon. That is what makes criticism of new ideas so damaging: at this particular moment, the critic is backed up by reality and the accepted truths of the profession, the group or even the whole of society. If the critic also happens to be in a position of power, the idea will be dead and buried before it's even been born. That is how vulnerable ideas are in the evaluation phase – no matter how successful they might prove to be in the end. Pessimists are closer to reality because they make their judgments based on their past experiences and the current rules derived from those experiences; optimists, on the other hand, think of the future and focus on the potential ramifications of a new idea. When we speak of reality, we mean the sum total of experiences, rules and customs on which the majority of the group or of society have agreed. But how can you evaluate the ideas of tomorrow if you have created them within the structures of today and are judging them by the standards of yesterday?

The so-called realists reveal themselves – often without knowing it – to be defenders of those old ideas that have so far managed to resist the advance of the modern age. Thinking in terms of new opportunities is therefore an invaluable talent, and if you haven't yet learned how to do it, you should disqualify yourself from the evaluation process straight away. This is not an appeal for naivety, of course, but a vital step on the way to innovation. Here are two more gems. In 1926, Lee de Forest, an early electronics pioneer, is said to have declared: 'While theoretically and technically television may be feasible, commercially and financially it is an impossibility.' His foresight was capped by the acuity of Avery Brundage, fifth president of the International Olympic Committee, who said: 'The IOC has managed without TV for sixty years and believe me – we are going to manage for another sixty.'

Credits Worldwide Pillow Fight Club 2009 – Vancouver, Canada | Photo Kevin Wu

▲ **Strategy:** This pillow fight flash mob was organized online and became a worldwide phenomenon covering more than 30 cities. With apparent spontaneity, people gather at a specified place at a specified time, to hold a gigantic pillow fight. In New York alone, some five thousand people took part.

Talking point: What might have prevented these events from being a success? Have a bit of fun: think up as many reasons as possible for not staging them.

▶ **Strategy:** At the Design Council Festival, Richard Liddle created chairs out of waste plastic that visitors brought with them. The waste was melted down into long plastic strips that could be moulded into any shape.

Talking point: Write down a list of all the criticisms you've used in recent years to attack or kill off someone else's ideas. Can you see a pattern in your arguments?

Credits Cohda Studio/Richard Liddle

THE 100 IDEAS DILEMMA

Imagine that your team has developed a huge pool of ideas. Can you explain how you'll be able to recognize the right one when you see it?

If an ideas meeting has gone really well, many of the participants will feel overwhelmed when they're confronted by masses of rough ideas. If there are over 100, this can induce a feeling of paralysis rather than of pleasure at having such a wide choice. This is perfectly natural, because generally we find it a strain to make decisions. Imagine having to choose one mountain bike from a range of 140 models – would your eyes light up or mist over? Even if we finally manage to single out idea no. 50, very often we don't feel entirely satisfied, and get a niggling feeling that maybe idea no. 91 was better after all. A large number of ideas also means a lot of work – developing, evaluating and selecting them costs time and nervous energy, not to mention money. This often causes a paradoxical reaction: people start to ask whether it would be better to develop, say, ten or twenty ideas, which would give a better overview and make selection easier. Indeed many creatives would rather sacrifice the chance to hit on one great idea than be exposed to the stress of considering hundreds. But it doesn't have to be a stressful process, so long as you take a systematic approach to your raw ideas pool. The whole situation becomes much more manageable when you've established clear parameters to help you take your decision. That is why, prior to evaluation or selection, you should always sit down with the client and use the brief as a basis to draw up a list of criteria that will allow you to decide on the ideas that will make it through to the next round.

▶ **Strategy:** Häagen Dazs invited 100 couples to a 'Dolce Heavenly Concert' with three world-class soloists. The guests watched the show from comfortable beds with lashings of delicious ice cream.

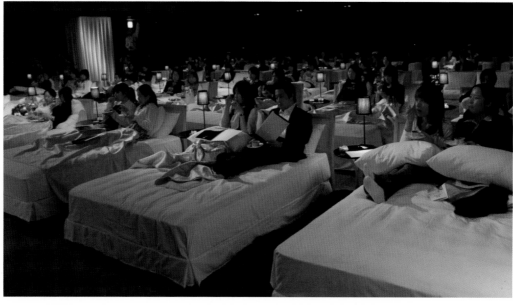

Talking point: Would you scrap an idea such as this one to avoid the stress of sorting through a vast pool? If you're only prepared to consider a handful of ideas, you could be leaving the most brilliant ones undiscovered – or simply pretending they don't exist.

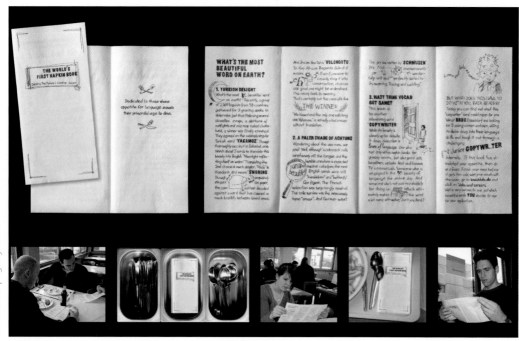

◀ **Strategy:** The advertising agency BBDO wanted to recruit talented copywriters from students who were studying German, and so they developed *The World's First Napkin Book*. It was handed out in student canteens together with the food, and introduced them to the glamorous world of advertising.

GROUPS WANT TO 'DO THE RIGHT THING'

If you feel happiest with mediocre, risk-free ideas, you should involve as many people as possible in the evaluation process. But if you're looking for really original ideas, it's best if only a few people make the selection.

During the evaluation phase, everyone involved ought to delete the words 'good' and 'sensible' from their vocabulary. These generally denote something that's just average and is already familiar from their own experiences. It's also very rare that ideas with the potential to actually create change can be called 'sensible' right from the start. And so somebody who wants to be good and sensible will automatically throw away anything original, and will assemble as large a team as possible of those who have already made up their minds to play safe. What sort of ideas do you think will survive this filtering process? New ideas are those that deviate from the norm, and that means that at first they may not seem right. But the more people you involve, the more likely it is that the group dynamic will drive them towards the conventional. It's common knowledge that the larger the group, the more the individuals merge together to form one big nobody. Every additional person taking part will create a drop in drive and initiative, and everyone will end up trying to outdo each other in their eagerness to 'do the right thing' – i.e. stick with the tried and trusted. Therefore it's vital to have someone with the courage and the power to make illogical decisions and avoid clichés. Ideas that deviate from the norm will generally only have a chance of survival if there is an individual or a small group prepared to break the mould.

▲ **Strategy:** To mark Barbie's 50th birthday, Fiat created one-off Fiat 500 in bright pink. It was designed jointly by Centro Stile Fiat and Mattel™. The interior, the wheel rims and even the aerial are decorated with crystals. The metallic pink of the chassis is echoed in the interior, and the seats are upholstered with two-colour Alcantara fabrics.

Talking point: The reason why so many successful ideas make a huge impact is that they deviate from the norm. If so far you haven't been able to prevent large teams from opting for what's 'right' – i.e. conventional – then start trying to find ways to persuade them to go against the grain.

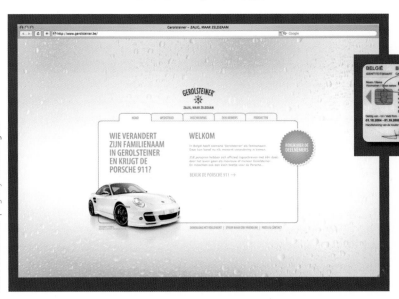

▲ **Strategy:** The German mineral water brand Gerolsteiner was completely unknown in Belgium, and so the agency devised a campaign to spread brand awareness. No one in Belgium had the surname Gerolsteiner, and so the first person to change their name by deed poll to Gerolsteiner won a brand new Porsche 911.

261

◀ **Strategy:** The name of the product is written using the product itself, instead of being printed on the packaging.

Talking point: How many departments or individuals do you think you would need to involve in the decision-making process to ensure that an idea like this one never had a chance?

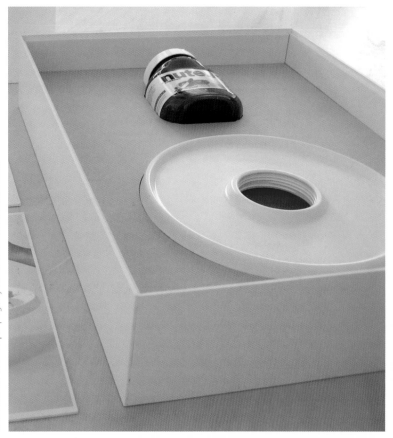

◀ **Strategy:** This tray attachment for Nutella jars won a contest run by Nutella and *Interni* magazine. It is easy to put on and take off, and allows party-goers to enjoy the delights of fruit and Nutella combined.

'Is that meant to be new? I've never seen anything like it!'

A marketing director

On first viewing, radically original ideas often lead clients to experience a state of shock: they gasp for breath, their eyes roll, and they are – momentarily – lost for words. It's not difficult to understand why: this is the first time they've seen an idea that the team has been working on for weeks, and they haven't had a chance to familiarize themselves step by step with the concept, or to get involved in the creative process so that they themselves might make a useful contribution. The creatives may have meant well – they only wanted to surprise the clients with their dazzlingly brilliant proposal. Instead, they present them with a shock. Presentations entail taking the lead, controlling the thoughts and expectations of everyone in attendance. Has it ever occurred to you to ask beforehand exactly what the client's expectations, values, wishes or fears might be? Your first step should be to take clients out of their own world and bring them into the new one which houses your idea. Every presentation should be uniquely tailored to suit its clients.

If you can't bring yourself to see things through their eyes, don't be surprised when they refuse to see things through yours during the presentation.

Presenting means taking the lead. A great presentation should be emotional and the sheer enthusiasm of your team should come across to everyone present. A word of warning, however: don't unleash your whole pack of party tricks just to palm off an idea on your clients. If they feel you're putting them under undue pressure, you'll simply lose credibility as well as their trust. Your concern here is to establish a long-term relationship of mutual trust and cooperation – not just to gain short-term success with a good presentation. Never lose sight of the fact that the idea itself must have the potential to grab their enthusiasm. When they see it, there should be an almost immediate spark, and if this happens, you will have massively increased your chances that the idea will have the same effect out on the open market, carrying the spark from one enthusiastic customer to another.

▼ **Strategy:** The character of the 'Bandito' was invented to promote Tesco Tortilla Chips. His outfit and appearance change to suit each flavour.

Talking point: Get your creative team to develop original ideas for presentations, and treat this as an integral feature of every project. What kind of presentation could you offer for this packet of potato chips? Think of every aspect: time, space, media, participants, dress, language and more.

Better leave your pet at home. Call 0900-2007 207

PET&BREAKFAST
DIERENPENSION
AMSTERDAM

▲ Strategy:
Print campaign for
the Pet & Breakfast
boarding kennels.

Talking point: When the screenplay for *King Kong* was first written, a Hollywood
executive is reputed to have said: 'Great story and we'd love to produce the film,
but we'll have to replace the gorilla with an animal that people like.' How can you
structure a successful presentation if you know in advance that your work goes
against the values, preconceptions and personal tastes of the client?

Having an idea is not enough. Only a great implementation of the idea will get people excited. To do this, you need two types of creativity: first to come up with a great idea, and secondly to implement this idea with unprecedented brilliance.

Many people think creativity ends after evaluation, when the right idea has been selected. After that, it's simply a matter of racing against the clock to get the first designs down on the drawing board. The fact that implementation also requires a great deal of creativity tends to escape the team until they are confronted with the fact that their brilliant idea has lost all its dazzle and has gone out into the world as just another campaign or product that will vanish in the crowd. Or perhaps it might still be good, but will it be good enough to really grab the target group? If you even have to ask that question, you should go straight back to square one and start all over again, or alternatively face up to the truth – you're never going to hit the heights as a creative.

Implementation depends on the skills of illustrators, designers, editors, photographers, copywriters and other artists from all creative fields. Their basic task is to give the idea its perfect shape, so that its sheer quality will stun the world and make everyone rush out to buy the product. Choosing the right people with the right skills is therefore crucial to the success of the project, and compromise in this field is absolutely forbidden. In the words of the great French writer Michel de Montaigne, 'Contentment is a great incentive to mediocrity.' The difference between an average creative department and a great one lies mainly in attention to detail. Whether you need a special effects scene, a strapline or a button for a designer jacket, true star performers will come up with not just one but dozens of alternatives. Okay is never good enough. The leading lights of the creative industries have a clear and simple policy: only the best, and to hell with the rest.

▲ Strategy:
This trade stand displays
the winter collection of
the BÄUMLER fashion
house in a wintery
landscape made up
of large-scale cutouts.

Talking point: How can you tell if the implementation of an idea has reached creative and qualitative perfection?
Many people are quite happy to stop short, although there are also some who go on too long and wreck the results
through overelaboration. For instance, a lot of the functions of Microsoft Office software are never used, and yet
they keep adding new ones. Would you say that this trade stand is as good as it could possibly be?

CREATIVE SPACES

06

SPACES CAN AFFECT THE CREATIVE CLIMATE

Sometimes how you're creative is less important than where you're creative. What kind of atmosphere and environment will stimulate a team's creativity and help to bring its ideas to life?

Even today there are certain places that are not only more inspirational than others, but are also more conducive to the survival of unusual ideas. Cities like Shanghai, New York, Berlin, Tokyo and London are veritable breeding grounds for new developments and global trends. The atmosphere in those places positively welcomes innovation, and this in itself hugely increases the chances of success. It also attracts top creatives and visionaries from all over the world, and the result is a positive feedback loop: the warm creative climate attracts more and more star performers, and their brilliant ideas make the creative climate even warmer, which attracts even more star performers, and so on. This effect is not confined to cities and regions – it also applies to buildings, rooms, and even individual workstations. Leave your office desk for a moment or two and have a look round the area in which your company is situated. Which are the places that seem to foster a genuinely creative atmosphere?

▶ Do you find your town creatively inspiring?
▶ Is your particular area an inspirational melting pot?
▶ Are there inspiring companies within the same street or building as yours?
▶ Does your office inspire creativity?
▶ Do the individual rooms inspire creativity?
▶ Does your desk inspire creativity?

▲ **Strategy:** For Pallotta TeamWorks, an event-planning and fundraising firm, Clive Wilkinson filled a warehouse covering an area of 4,000 m² with shipping containers that form offices for the whole team. As the containers can be stacked one on top of another, this provides an unusual and extremely effective use of space.

Talking point: Office spaces can turn into a kind of island, with its own particular microclimate. How could you design an office so that on the one hand it reflects the needs of the company, independently of what is happening in the world outside, and on the other hand produces a stimulating, creative atmosphere?

▲ **Strategy:** This church in Leatherhead, Surrey, has been converted into open-plan offices. Anyone renting a space here will share it with companies in many different fields, but all of them will benefit from the stimulating environment of Gothic architecture, stained glass windows, oak panelling and solid wooden floors.

▶ Strategy: The London-based agency group known as Engine combines twelve companies under a single roof. The offices were designed by Jump Studios, and try to cater for all tastes and cultures without ever losing sight of the corporate identity.

Client **Engine** | Agency **Jump Studios**

Photo © Siemens Press Picture

Imagine an agency that has assigned a totally white conference room to you and your colleagues. Their reasoning is that new ideas can only emerge from an environment with no distractions and no outside influences. What effect might this have on the flow of images that creatives bring with them to the office every day?

First things first: there is no universal formula to determine how offices or even workstations should be designed to get the best out of the people who work there. Different creatives work in different ways, and so ideally the design should adapt to reflect every individual's requirements and personal taste. What people often forget is the fact that we can be stimulated through all five senses: sight, hearing, touch, smell and taste.

If you take a closer look at a conventional conference room, you'll see that at best it might provide a few visual stimuli, but the other senses are completely ignored. That's a pity, because each of the senses sparks off a different part of the brain, thereby creating a much wider variety of associations. The question therefore arises as to whether rooms could be designed using new technologies and materials in order to give an extra kick to the creative processes. If you like the idea of exploring new territory, why not experiment with your surroundings and add a little extra spice to office life? Imagine the effect if your meeting rooms were regularly transformed through different sensory experiences and an ever-changing creative atmosphere.

Talking point: When was the last time you thought about your environment as an active element in the creative process? Seen through the eyes of a child, how should your office be designed in order to stimulate all the senses and help people to become totally absorbed in whatever task they are doing?

▶ **Strategy:** The London-based advertising agency Langland provides its creatives with several areas that invite leisurely communication as well as creating a stimulating environment.

Talking point: In what ways could the less 'official' places like the kitchen, corridors or even toilets be designed to provide more stimulation for the senses?

▶ **Strategy:** The new Google offices in Zürich were designed entirely in accordance with the wishes of the workers. They offer plenty of space for communication, attractive recreation rooms, a library, a fitness centre, a massage centre, and a rest room with an aquarium.

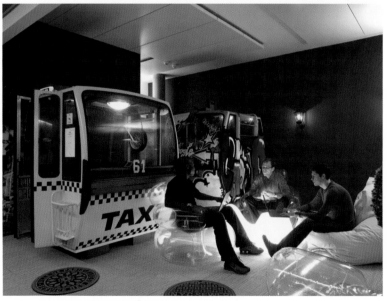

Client **Google** | Agency **Camenzind Evolution**, Architecture – Design – Technology

Talking point: When planning a creative department, you need to provide for relaxation as well as stimulation. Many creatives tend to be introspective, and use their own thoughts and images as an archive to draw on for inspiration. Outside stimuli can often be regarded as a disturbance. There are others, however, who actually seek out external sensory stimuli and need them to set their creative gears in motion. Both groups should be able to find areas in your office that suit their particular needs.

WHEN ECCENTRICITY BECOMES THE NORM

Ideally, the offices of a creative agency should focus on two areas: creation and implementation.

When you look at the weird and wonderful offices of some creative agencies, you can't help feeling that the design is more for the benefit of their corporate image than for the people who actually work there. However, it's worth asking precisely what those people need. In my experience, they require a space in which they can not only be creative but also find the staying power to take original ideas right through to implementation. Between these two poles lie a wide range of needs, and so if you are planning to build brand new premises, you could start by using the creativity of your teams to find out what they think would be ideal surroundings for them. They might want a room with a large touchscreen, so that all the participants at a meeting can submit their ideas via the office Intranet and use them as a basis for discussion. Or maybe a soundproof room in which loud music can be played during the design phase. You could also include a fitness centre, since people sometimes get ideas when they're on the move. Some walls could be designed so that they can be drawn on, or used to display sketches or printouts. How about incorporating a kind of padded cell – not for tantrums, but for all kinds of materials used to express all kinds of messages, and at the end of the meeting it can be hosed down so that it's nice and clean for the next session?

Compile a detailed list of the team's requirements before you commission a designer – remember, form follows function. There are plenty of offices that look cool or impressive to visitors but aren't conducive to anything but work. And always keep in mind that even the craziest of rooms will eventually become a familiar and hence normal environment, and this familiarity will neutralize the stimulating effects that were originally intended to inspire its occupants. You could even ask whether it would make more sense to create an ever-changing environment for your creatives. How would the workplace look if the design had to be able to change regularly, and what new technologies could be utilized in order to counter the stultifying effects of daily routines, fixed structures and over-familiarity?

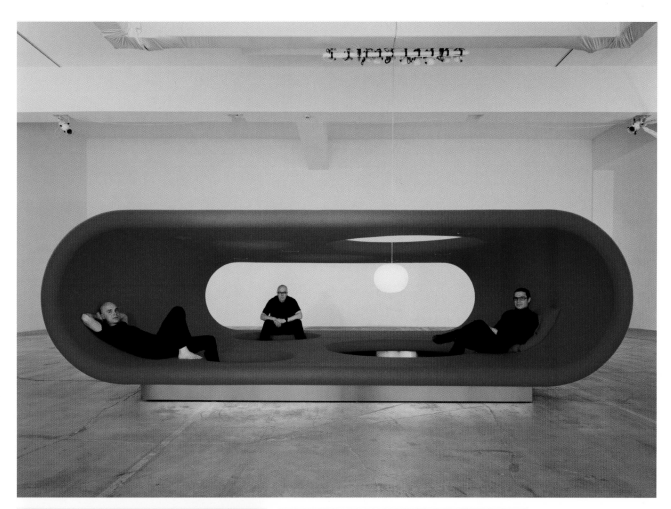

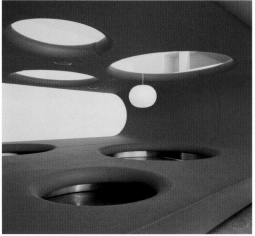

▲ **Strategy:** The Luna was developed by Swedish design house Claesson Koivisto Rune. But what is it? It could be described as a simple piece of furniture, a playground for creatives, and a new style of conference room, all in one.

Talking point: Spaces that deviate from the norm are a reminder to their occupants that they are meant to be creative. Teams should work in places that constantly remind them that they can do things here that they couldn't do anywhere else.

▲ **Strategy:** The British firm Inflate produces lightweight, transportable rooms and fittings that can be inflated and so seem to spring up out of nowhere. In next to no time you can erect chill-out zones, conference rooms, offices or bars, and then make them disappear just as quickly.

Talking point: Creativity implies constant instability and change. If you want to encourage creativity in your team, you must meet their need for personal stability and security while at the same time avoiding any rigid structures that might lead to a loss of flexibility. Try to design rooms that offer a continuous flow of stimuli and challenges, keeping your creatives alert and adaptable.

Client **Kvadrat A/S** | Design **Ronan and Erwan Bouroullec**

▲ Strategy: 'Clouds' is a modular system designed by the brothers Ronan and Erwan Bouroullec in conjunction with Kvadrat. The elements are covered with coarse fabric and can be attached to one another with Velcro. The deliberate avoidance of rectangular shapes ensures that when the pieces are joined in a group, they always take on a three-dimensional form. When used in large quantities, these 'clouds' can be used as unusual room dividers, wall decorations or screens.

Talking point: Whether it's a huge open-plan office or a small workroom, how can your working environment be adapted to suit the individual needs of your team members?

Credits Patrick Blanc

▲ **Strategy:** Patrick Blanc combines architecture and plants as elements of exterior and interior design. This vertical garden is the result of his close observation of nature which led him to the idea of getting plants to grow on vertical surfaces. These green areas make for an optimal microclimate, balanced humidity, less dust, and a reduction in CO_2 emissions.

Talking point: Most offices are full of signs and symbols which subconsciously influence people's behaviour and can lead to a normative way of thinking: conference table, collar and tie, video projector, fluorescent strip lighting, flipcharts, Post-It notes. Could you find ways of disrupting the routine by replacing these 'symptoms' with something totally new?

▲ **Strategy:** The offices of the Chicago-based firm skinnyCorp give their workers plenty of space, in an environment that provides them with lots of aids to communication, and a relaxing atmosphere with diversions such as pinball machines, pool tables, flatscreen TVs and computer games.

Talking point: How can you prevent even the most innovative office from eventually becoming familiar and gradually losing its power to stimulate?

Talking point: When sitting at a desk, you spend most of your time with your body in the same position, and surrounded by the same environment. What features could potentially be included in a workplace that would allow it to offer new possibilities instead of limiting them?

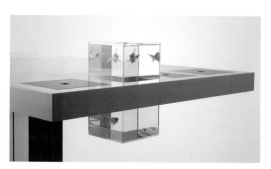

Credits **Robert Scales/Raincity Studios**

Credits **BBDO**

Photo **twoeyes**

CREATIVITY HAPPENS WHEN YOU MAKE SPACE FOR IT

Ideas are not bound to particular places, so why should you stay in the office? Thinking outside the box is sometimes most successful when you leave the box that you work in every day.

Even the major international agencies are gradually changing the design of their offices. Consider all the possibilities that are on offer today: the world of work can be totally revolutionized in terms of hours, procedures and geographical locations. For instance, you could have a flexible workplace, with teams changing over every week. Or you could go a step further and start up small creative cells that move from place to place with a maximum of, say, 35 people in each one. According to the demands of each project, teams or individuals could switch between cells. There are already many designers who say their workplace is wherever they are at any given moment. With the aid of modern technology, it's become relatively simple for teams to swap places and to decide for themselves what surroundings would be best for them to work in. No matter whether you're in a sterile cubicle in an open-plan office building, the canteen, a restaurant, your study, a park, or a rented workshop inside some other, unrelated company – inspiration can come to you anywhere. However, despite this vast range of opportunities, you must never lose sight of one vital factor: the goal of having a flexible workplace and flexible working procedures. Your aim should be to keep your team stimulated, get rid of the old and outdated structures, open the door to new impulses from outside, and promote cooperation and motivation from within.

▲ **Strategy:** For the launch of the Tube Carriage Office in London, disused train carriages were hoisted into position on the roof of a building to provide a striking working environment for creative start-ups.

Talking point: Small creative cells are generally flexible enough for people to change their working environment occasionally without much expense. What effect might it have on a creative team if it changed its address every so often in order to give itself fresh impetus?

287

▲ Strategy: The Montreal-based agency Sid Lee opened up a branch in Amsterdam which calls itself a 'gallery-boutique-atelier'. With a name like that, it's not altogether surprising that apart from creating ad campaigns, the agency runs its own designer store, café and gallery.

Talking point: What would happen if you jettisoned the concept of the traditional office, and linked it to other fields, introducing ideas that would revolutionize how people think of agencies and offices?

▲ **Strategy:** La Oficina in Copenhagen has offices for rent that are highly unconventional. A large bar, a grand piano and the layout of the workplaces themselves suggest the designer flair of a large coffee house rather than a typical office building. Which buildings or rooms in your immediate surroundings could be converted in this way?

Talking point: Would it be possible for you to regularly hold creative meetings outside of your own agency? Which buildings or spaces nearby could be used for this purpose?

▲ **Strategy:** Nissan's NV200 concept car was inspired by a professional underwater photographer. It contains a cargo pod with drawers and compartments for equipment, and when this slides out, the van becomes a mobile office. It could of course be modified for other users.

Talking point: People sometimes get their ideas in the unlikeliest of places: on the motorway, in the train, on their bike, or while they're on holiday. Why shouldn't we make this phenomenon part of our standard practice, and send small creative teams off on a journey somewhere?

SPACES AS CREATIVE PLAYGROUNDS

Ideally, anyone stepping into unknown territory will know their destination, but will probably not know the best route to get there. It is this very uncertainty that makes it essential to have spaces that invite creative experimentation.

Developing something new means setting out on a quest without knowing what exactly you're looking for or where you'll find it. Even if creative teams have been given a precisely formulated goal, they do not have a detailed route map to guide them into new territory within the realms of, say, design, packaging, film, fashion or product development. To outside eyes, it might often seem that their approach to the task is neither logical nor even serious. They have to experiment if they are to innovate, and this process is almost always guided by instincts and feelings, and certainly not by conventional rules or past successes. One very common sign of a new discovery is a deepening feeling of insecurity. You are suddenly in unknown territory, and you can't refer to a map to help you find the way. That is why creatives need a protected space with clear parameters, and a realistic timeframe that will allow them to try out different routes, most of which will usually turn out to be blind alleys. Unfortunately, this kind of latitude and playful freedom is an element that many agencies these days feel unable to allow. The result is almost invariably the need to repeat ideas, or dress old successes in new colours and pretend they're original. But there are a number of modern research labs, colleges and universities that can show us how to construct 'play areas', and you will find a few genuinely inspirational ideas on the pages that follow.

▲ Strategy: Students at the Eindhoven Design Academy are encouraged to use the extensive play areas for their personal 'research projects', rather than treading the paths of their predecessors.

Talking point: If a student from the Eindhoven Design Academy joined your team, how long would it take for her to abandon her own creative style and way of working in order to fit in with the current structures of your company? How could you prevent her fresh and uninhibited approach from melting away in her new surroundings and with her new colleagues?

► Strategy:
Fabrica is a centre for communications research that was founded in 1994 by the Benetton Group. Its aim is to link industry and culture through communications by combining classic forms of advertising with other modes of expression: design, music, film, photography, editing software, the internet. Fabrica is an investment in the untapped creativity of youth as well as that of experimental artists from all over the world, who have been specially chosen and invited to develop concrete communications projects in different fields.

▲ **Strategy:** The Fashion Institute of Design & Merchandise in Los Angeles offers its students a studio designed by Clive Wilkinson Architects.

The goal is to offer tools, materials and facilities that will encourage students to try out new ideas in the various fields they hope to work in.

Talking point: If you compare the conference rooms and creative 'play areas' in your own company with those illustrated here, what can you learn that might improve your creative climate in the long term?

APPENDIX

© Christian Postl

Christine Klell
Design and concept
Christine Klell is a designer, creativity trainer and guest lecturer at a design school. For more than a decade she has used her distinctive design talents on a wide range of books in a huge variety of styles. She is also Mario Pricken's long-time partner and colleague and has worked as a trainer since 2004, enhancing the creativity of teams across the creative industries. In addition to giving this book its unmistakable look, she also worked on *Creative Advertising* and *Visual Creativity* (as designer and co-author).
www.christine-klell.com

Mina Mahmudi
Picture research and project management
Mina Mahmudi studied for her BA in Management and Marketing at Webster University in Vienna. For several years, she made use of her language talents at a translation agency. She is now studying for a MA in Innovation Management at Central Saint Martins College of Art and Design in London. For this book, she worked as project manager and organized the picture research. Her multicultural background and communication skills were the perfect match for the whole project.
project@mariopricken.com

Max Julian Otto
Illustration
Max Julian Otto is a freelance illustrator and set designer. His speciality is the field of film illustration, concept art and storyboards. In the course of his career to dae, he has worked on more than 500 ads and TV and cinema productions. This book has been given a boost by his wonderful hand-drawn illustrations.
www.max-julian-otto.de

Christian Anderl
Photography
Christian Anderl has been a presenter on Austria's top radio station for almost a decade. Further from the public eye, however, he also produces professional work in two other fields: photography and video art. As well as taking great photographs, he has worked on several successful music videos and other video projects. This book showcases his multifaceted talents as a photographer.
www.christiananderl.com

Ilze Filmanovica
Press Officer
Ilze Filmanovica grew up in the Latvian capital Riga and graduated with a BA in Intercultural Relations. She worked at the PR agency Deep White as a project leader for two years. She is currently studying for an MA in Public Communication at the University of Vienna.
press@mariopricken.com

Title: *1 vs. 100*
Client: Magic Media Company
Technical realization: Procon Event
Engineering GmbH

Client: 3M Earplugs
Title: 'Plug In' Calendar
Agency: BUTTER. Düsseldorf
Creative directors: Matthias Eickmeyer,
Michael Preuss
Art director: Nadine Schlichte
Copywriters: Stefan Mattes, Julia Kaminski
Photographer: Franklin Berger

A
Client: Adidas AG
Title: mi Adidas Innovation Center, Paris
Design: Mutabor Design
Art directors: Heinrich Paravicini,
Axel Domke
Designers: Thomas Huth, Christan Tönsmann,
Andreas Schradin, Ksawery Oroczko
Photographer: Andreas Keller

Client: AIDA Cruises
Title: *AIDAdiva* ship launch, Hamburg
Directed by: Get Hof
Technical realization:
PROCON Event Engineering
Photographer: Ralph Larmann

Client: Akzo Nobel Paints Belgium nv
Title: Levis, Ambiance
Agency: TBWA\Brussels
Photographer: Kurt Stallaert;
www.kurtstallaert.com

Client: Amnesty International
Title: Amnesty Candle
Agency: Air Brussels, Belgium
Creative director: Veronique Sels
Art director: Anthony Hirschfeld
Copywriter: Veronique Sels
Photographer: Abbas @ Magnum Photos

Client: Amway India
Title: 'Chicken'
Agency: Rediffusion Young & Rubicam,
Gurgaon, India
Product: Persona Toothbrush
Executive creative directors:
Ramanuj Shastry, Sagar Mahabaleshwar
Creative directors: Abhinav Pratiman,
Daniel Upputuru
Art director: Rishi Chanana
Copywriter: Abhinav Pratiman
Photographer: Jasmer Singh

Client: Amway Thailand
Title: 'Beatle'
Agency: Y&R Bangkok
Product: Amway Silicone Glaze Car Polish
Executive creative directors:
Trong Tantivejakul, Marcus Rebeschini
Art director: Nares Limapornvanich
Copywriters: Jittra Thiuthipsakul,
Denchai Kererug
Photographer: Boonsunh Chalard
Image composer: Presto
Agency producer: Amornmarn
Rattanarakpinyo
Production house: Sunhouse

Credits: Apple, Inc.
Title: Apple Design

Client: Arcor
Title: '3D Ball'
Product: Big Big Bubble Gum
Agency: Leo Burnett Publicidade Ltda,
Brazil
Chief creative officer: Ruy Lindenberg
Art director: Luis Catapano

Client: Arge Pilot
Title: 'Goldfish'
Agency: Grey Barcelona
Executive creative director: Jürgen Krieger
Creative directors: Joan Más,
José Miguel Tortajada, Alex Martin
Art directors: Dani Páez, Saül Serradesanferm,
Oscar Amodia
Copywriters: Aitor Borras, Jorge Meneclier,
Alberto Ramos

Client: Armila
Title: Garmastan 'Torn Nipple'
Agency: MILK

Client: Asian Paints Ltd.
Title: 'Glow Paint – Cinderella'
Agency: Ogilvy & Mather, Mumbai
Executive creative director: Piyush Pandey
Creative directors: Abhijit Avasthi,
Shekhar Jha, Mahesh Gharat
Art directors: Makarand Joshi,
Santosh Walwaikar
Copywriters: Shekhar Jha, Arshad Sardar
Illustrator: Dnyanesh Parab
Designers: Makarand Joshi, Mahesh Gharat

Client: Audi
Title: SPORE Audi Design Competition
Idea: Jörg Brand (product marketing manager,
Electronic Arts GmbH), Kai Mensing (online
marketing, Audi AG)
Technical realization/creation of the online
special: neue digitale/razorfish, Berlin

Credits: Autodesk/The Grove Consultants
International
Title: TED 2008 BIGVIZ Sketchbook
Project by: David Sibbet, Kevin Richards

Client: AVRO
Title: *The Phone*
Agency: New Message Amsterdam
Copywriter: Hugo Rütter
Art director: Lennart Wienecke

B

Client: BASF SE
Agency: circ gmbh & co. kg
Title: pack.it.2006, 'La Réflexion du Fond'
Project director: Stephan Pachner
Creative director: Hans Reitz
Art director: Xavier Juillot

Client: BÄUMLER
Title: Bäumler/Pitti Summer 2006
Design firm: ARNO Design GmbH
Design: Mirka Nassiri, Claus Neuleib,
Peter Haberlander
Photographer: Frank Kotzerke

Client: BBDO
Title: 'The World's First Napkin Book'
Agency: BBDO Düsseldorf GmbH
Creative directors: Toygar Bazarkaya,
Sebastian Hardieck, Ralf Zilligen
Art directors: Lidia Pranjic, Caroline Kunsemüller
Copywriters: Helmut Bienfuss,
Douglas Tracy, Yvette Bradley
Client consultant: Bianca Scheiwe
Agency producer: Bernhard Burg
Photographer: Jost Hiller
Illustration: Lidia Pranjic
Production: Engelmann Druckerei

Client: Black Tulip Amsterdam
Title: 'Floormap'
Agency: Euro RSCG Amsterdam, Netherlands
Art director: Gijs van den Berg
Copywriter: Niek Eijsbouts

Credits: Patrick Blanc
Title: Vertical Garden

Client: Brighton Language School
Title: 'Deutsch', 'English'
Agency: Voskhod, Yekaterinburg, Russia
Creative director: Andrey Gubaydullin
Art director: Vlad Derevyannykh
Copywriters: Aleksandr Parkhomenko,
Evgeny Primachenko
Photographer: Vyacheslav Lvov
Illustrator and designer: Dimitry Maslakov

Client: Bosch
Title: 'Lawnmower' direct mail
Agency: Jung von Matt, Hamburg
Executive creative directors:
Wolf Heumann, Dirk Häusermann,
Timm Hanebeck, Sascha Hanke
Art directors: Andy Tran, Hendrik Schweder
Graphic designer: Nadya Innamorato
Agency producer: Philipp Wenhold

Title: *The Buried Life*
Team: Duncan Penn, Jonnie Penn,
Dave Lingwood, Ben Nemtin
Executive producer/manager: Jan Coleman

Client: BYE HELMETS
Title: 'Hands'
Agency: 1861UNITED
Executive creative directors: Pino Rozzi,
Roberto Battaglia
Copywriter: Luca Beato
Art director: Giorgio Cignoni
Photographer: Fulvio Bonavia

C

Client: Casinò di Venezia
Title: 'Keep Playing'
Agency: AdmCom
Creative director: Maurizio Cinti
Art directors: Sergio Lelli, Andrea Ligi

Title: The Chapel, Leatherhead
Company: The Chapel
Creative agency: Phoenix Plc
www.thechapelsurrey.com

Title: 'Choco' experimental packaging
Credits: Petar Pavlov

Credits: Claesson Koivisto Rune
Title: Luna
Designers: Mårten Claesson,
Eero Koivisto, Ola Rune
Assistant designer: Patrick Coan
Manufacturer: Dune (USA);
www.dune-ny.com

Client: Colgate – Palmolive (Thailand) Ltd.
Title: 'Remind'
Agency: Y&R Thailand
Product: Colgate Toothbrush
Executive creative director: Marcus Rebeschini
Creative directors: Noppadol Utiswannakul
Art director: Kijchapon Patiwongphaisarn,
Somchok Kunjaethong
Photographers: Jasda Trivittayanuruk,
Yoothana Sasanatiang
Account services: Jaime Prieto, Sanjay Bhasin,
Ittawin Ngoenwichit, Natphon Pholsong
Agency producer: Amornmarn
Rattanarakpinyo
Production house: Fiftyone

Client: California Milk Processor Board
Title: 'Get the Glass'
Agency: North Kingdom
Lead agency: Goodby, Silverstein & Partners

Client: Coca-Cola
Title: Coke Zero Table Football
Agency: Leo Burnett, Budapest
Executive creative director: Vilmos Farkas
Art directors: Miklos Voros, Matyas Kobor
Creative director: Peter Tordai
Copywriter: Linda Zador

Client: Coca-Cola
Title: Coca-Cola Multimedia Vending Machine
Design: Sapient/Samsung

Client: Coca-Cola Germany
Title: Coca-Cola Zero
Agency: North Kingdom

Client: Concave Scream
Title: Concave Scream Horizons
Agency: Kinetic Singapore
Creative directors: Pann Lim, Roy Poh
Art directors: Leng Soh, Pann Lim, Roy Poh
Illustrators: Andy Yang, Sean Lam

Client: CITY Magazine
Title: 'Dry Clean Only'
Photographer: Ted Sabarese
Styling: Laura Tiozzo
Make-up/hair: Marija Kopilas
Costumes: Nick Cave

Title: Creative Desk
Credits: Sander van den Dries
Zwolle – The Netherlands
www.x-media.nl

D

Designer: Daniel Loves Objects
Title: *Of Wars & Wits & Power*, bookcase

Client: Danone Group
Title: Jean Paul Gaultier Special Edition 2009
Product: Evian
Design: Jean Paul Gaultier

Title: *Dating in the Dark*
Format creation: John de Mol
Executive producer: Tom Shelly
Co-executive producer: Richard Devinki
Supervising producers: David Pritikin,
Karen Ripenburg, Johnny Petillo
Original format: Talpa Content B.V.
Licence: Talpa Distribution B.V.
Director of photography: Jim Harrington
Production designer: Jeff Hall

Client: Dell
Title: 'Towel Drop'
Agency: Mother Experience
Creative director: Tom Webster
Art director: Gui Burchert
Copywriter: Jon Lancaric
Producers: Mike Tooley, Brooke Wagner
Production company: Mother Experience

Client: Designboom and Procter & Gamble
'Reinvent' competition
Title: Mr Clean 'Dumb Bell'
Designers: Tommaso Ceschi,
Francesca Del Vigo

Client: Diesel
Title: Diesel Liquid Space Show
Creative director: Wilbert Das (Diesel)
Technology: Vizoo & Seelite
Visual effects and animation: Dvein

Client: Discovery Channel
Title: 'Alaska Week'
Supervising producer: Valerie Carrillo
Production manager: Kevin Lahr
Art director: Amie Nguyen
Creative director: Jeff Strong
VP creative: Dan Bragg
Design/production company: HUSH
Directors: David Schwarz & Erik Karasyk
Art director: Laura Alejo
Design: Graham Hill, Wes Ebelhar
Executive producer: Casey Steele
Producer: Jessica Le
Copywriter: Charles Short
2D animation: Elliot Blanchard, Bryan
Cobonpue, Salih Abdul-Karim, Wes Ebelhar
Roto artist: James Fitzpatrick
3D modelling and animation:
Scott Denton, Orges Kokoshari
3D lighting and texture: Matthew Wilson
Editors: Ian Ogden, Eli Mavros
Sound design/score: Antfood
Composers: Wilson Brown, Polly Hall
Executive producer: Sean McGovern

Client: Distell/Nederburg
Titel: Distell/Nederburg Ingenuity Wines:
'Spines'
Agency: Network BBDO

Title: Doodle Kids
Designed/programmed/written by:
Lim Ding Wen

Client: Dove
Title: 'Evolution'
Agency: Ogilvy & Mather, Toronto
Director: Yael Staav
Director/copywriter/art director: Tim Piper
Art director: Mike Kirkland
Creative directors: Janet Kestin, Nancy Vonk
Producer: Jennifer Walker
Production company: Reginald Pike
Animator: Kevin Gibson
Photographer: Gabor Jurina

Client: Durex
Title: Balloons
Agency: Fitzgerald + CO
Chief creative officer: Eddie Snyder
Creative directors: Jerry Williams,
Fernando Lecca
Copywriter: Jerry Williams
Art director: Fernando Lecca
Chief broadcast officer: Christine Sigety
Animation production: Superfad/New York
Executive producer: Geraint Owen
Creative director: Rob Rugan
Audio: Gramercy Post

E

Client: Eindhoven Design Academy
Title: Workshop for masters students at
De Fabriek (Eindhoven)
Photo: Niels Huneker
Title: Eindhoven/FRAME
Photographer: Daniel Nicolas;
www.danielnicolas.com

Client: Yiorgos Eleftheriades
Title: Renovation of the YEshop in-house
showroom
Design: dARCHstudio
(Elina Drossou Architects)
Architect: Elina Drossou
Collaborators: Nikos Karkatselas,
Chrysa Konstantinidou
Photographers: Vasilis Skopelitis,
Elina Drossou

Title: Emotional Cities
Concept: Erik Krikortz
Production: Erik Krikortz
Website, concept and design: Erik Krikortz
Website, design and concept: Farfar
Graphic design: Simon Mårtelius
Technical creation: Bo Gustavsson
Photographer: Åsa Lundén, Moderna Museet
www.emotionalcities.com

Client: Engine
Title: Engine Offices, London
Design: Jump Studios

Client: Expedia.com GmbH
Title: 'Weather Channel Guerrilla'
Agency: Serviceplan/Mediaplus
Executive creative directors:
Matthias Harbeck, Ekki Frenkler
Creative directors: Bernd Huesmann,
Sabine Hell
Chief creative officer: Alex Schill
Copywriters: Bernd Huesmann,
Michael Schulz, Hannah Nickl
Art directors: Christian Sommer, Ivo Hlavac

F

Credits: Fabrican spray-on fabric
Photographers: Gene Kiegel, Marc Broussely
www.fabricanltd.com

Client: Fashion Institute of Design
and Merchandise, Los Angeles
Design: Clive Wilkinson Architects

Client: FedEx
Title: FedEx Express
Agency: DM9 DDB, Brazil
Creative directors: Rodolfo Sampaio,
Julio Andery, Sergio Valente
Art director: Benjamin Yung Jr.
Copywriter: Arício Fortes
Photographer: Marcus Hausser

Client: Fiat
Title: Fiat 500 Interactive Poster
Agency: Leo Burnett, Frankfurt
Creative directors: Ulf Henniger von
Wallersbrunn, Andreas Stalder
Art director: Ulf Henniger von Wallersbrunn
Copywriter: Andreas Stalder
Executive creative director: Andreas Pauli
Associate executive creative director:
Kerrin Nausch

Client: Fiat Auto Argentina
Title: 'Warehouse', 'TV', 'Office'
Agency: Leo Burnett, Buenos Aires
Product: Fiat Adventure
Chief creative directors: Seto Olivieri,
Pablo Capara
Creative directors: Carmelo Maselli,
Luis Sanchez Zinny
Art directors: Ammiel Fazzari,
Carmelo Maselli
Copywriters: Juan Ignacio Galardi,
Matias Eusebi, Luis Sanchez Zinny
Account director: Hernán Cuñado
Agency photography producer:
Mariana Haxell
Photographer: Juan Mathé for argentinafoto
Retouching: Walter Becker

Credits: Fiat/Mattel™
Title: Fiat 500 Barbie®
Design: Centro Stile Fiat
Head of design: Roberto Giolito

Client: Fitness First
Title: Bus Stop
Agency: N=5
Creatives: Marco de Jong, Thijs Bontje,
Jurriaan Noij

Client: Fontegrafica
Creative firm: Cacao Design
Creative directors: Mauro Pastore,
Masa Magnoni, Alessandro Floridia
Designer: Paolo Sala
Printed by: Fontegrafica
www.fontegrafica.it

Client: Forus
Title: Columbia air conditioners
Agency: Prolam Y&R, Santiago
Creative director: Alvaro Becker
Art directors: Fabrizio Capraro,
Renzo Vaccaro

Title: Free Hugs Campaign
Credits: Juan Mann

Design: Front/Interactive Institute
Title: Flower Lamp
Design Research Project: 'STATIC!' (Interactive
Institute)
Funding: Swedish Energy Agency
Photographer: Interactive Institute
www.tii.se/projects/static

G
Client: Gahns
Title: Gahns – Soap on a Rope
Agency: Volt
Creative director: Mans Jacobsson Hosk
Art directors: Joakim Söderquist,
Mikael Söderblom
Copywriters: Jens Thelfer, Claes Olson

Client: Gerolsteiner
Title: 'Change Your Name'
Agency: MortierBrigade
Creative directors: Jens Mortier,
Joost Berends, Philippe De Ceuster
Copywriters/art directors:
Tim Driesen, Joeri Vandenbroeck

Client: Google
Title: Google Zurich Office
Design: Camenzind Evolution, Architecture –
Design – Technology
Executive director: Stefan Camenzind
Creative director: Tanya Ruegg-Basheva
Technical director: Marco Noch

Client: Guggenheim Bilbao Museoa
Title: 'The Art of the Motorcycle'
Design: Frank O. Gehry Associates
©FMGBGuggenheim Bilbao Museoa, 2009
Photographer: Erika Barahona Ede

H
Client: Häagen-Dazs Japan, Inc.
Title: 'Dolce Heavenly Concert'
Agency: Dentsu Inc.
Creative director: Tatsuyuki Hamada
(Drill Inc.)
Promotion producers: Shinji Okuno/Kohei
Aono (FRONTIER INTERNATIONAL INC.)
Production producers: Yasuo Deguchi/
Ryo Watanabe (HOSEISHA CO., LTD)
PR director: Jun Kawakami

Client: Harvey Nichols
Title: 'Vultures' sale campaign
Agency: DDB London
Creative director: Jeremy Craigen
Art director: Richard Denney
Copywriter: Dave Henderson

Client: Harvey Nichols
Title: Harvey Nichols Bristol Store Opening
'Wallace & Gromit' Campaign
Agency: DDB London
Creative director: Jeremy Craigen
Art director/copywriter: Grant Parker

Client: Hatari Electric Co., Ltd
Title: 'Skydiving' / 'Speedboat'
Product: Hatari Fan
Agency: Lowe Bangkok
Creative directors: Supon Khaotong,
Kittinan Sawasdee, Piya Churarakpong
Art directors: Porakit Tanwattana,
Asawin Techasakulsin
Copywriters: Noranit Yasopa,
Ekapol Srisuntornpinit
Cameraman: Srimongkol Phachonkaew
(Illusion)
Illustrator: Phutthiphong Yommasan (Illusion)
Image composer: Phutthiphong Yommasan
(Illusion)
Agency producer: Nutwithu Saengvichien
Production house: Illusion

Client: hauswein.de
Title: Packaging design
Company: Hayn/Willemeit Media GmbH
Strategic planning: Tobias Willemeit
Art direction: Markus Hayn
Web: Nils Kulinsky
Photographer: Stephan Klonk

Client: Heinz
Title: 'Dragon'
Product: Heinz Hot Ketchup
Agency: Leo Burnett, Brussels
Creative directors: Jean-Paul Lefebvre,
Michel De Lauw
Art director: Mathieu Dubray
Illustrator: Michel Denis – Victor 3D

Client: Help Remedies
Products: Help I Have a Headache/
Help I've Cut Myself
Design: Little Fury and Chapps Malina

Client: Henkel
Title: Pritt MyStyle
Product: Pritt
Agency: Waacs Design & Consultancy
Design by: Waacs Design Team

Title: 'Her Morning Elegance'
Co-director/songwriter: Oren Lavie
Co-directors/animators: Yuval and Merav
Nathan
Photographer: Eyal Landesman

Client: The Home Depot®
Title: HomeHero™ Fire Extinguisher
Company: Arnell Group, LLC

Client: Hut Weber
Title: 'Hitler vs. Chaplin'
Agency: Serviceplan München/Hamburg
Creative directors: Alexander Schill,
Axel Thomsen
Text/copywriter: Francisca Maass
Art directora: Jonathan Schupp, Imke Jurok
Account managers: Julia Thoemen,
Constanze Strothmann

I
Client: IKEA Germany
Agency: Jung von Matt AG
Title: IKEA 3D Cover
Creative directors: Arno Lindemann,
Bernhard Lukas, Tom Hauser, Soeren Porst
Art director: Joanna Swistowiski
Copywriters: Caroline Ellert, Tom Hauser
Computer animation: Sven Schoenmann
Graphic art: Matthias Grundner,
Julia Jakobi

Client: IKEA Germany
Title: IKEA 'Bigger Storage Ideas'
Agency: Ogilvy Frankfurt
Chief creative officer: Delle Krause
Creative directors: Thomas Hofbeck,
Lars Huvart
Art director: Kerstin Eberbach
Copywriter: Lars Huvart
Graphic designer: Kerstin Eberbach
Production: Fabian Schrader

Client: IKEA Japan
Title: Kobe Portliner Monorail
Design: IKEA Design

Client: IKEA Malaysia
Title: 'IKEA Shred, Peel, Slice'
Agency: Lowe & Partners Kuala Lumpur
Executive creative director: Ng Heok Seong
Art directors: Khor Kok Yang, Joseph Lee
Copywriter: Mohan Prabhakar
Designer: Lim Ken Peng
Photographer: Studio Pashe

Client: Illusion Labs AB
Title: Touchgrind
Designer: Mirabelle Looft
www.touchgrind.com

Client: illy
Title: illy Push Button House
Architect: Adam Kalkin
Photographer: © Peter Aaron/Esto
Photographics Inc.

Title: I Love My Country
Format creation: John de Mol
Executive producer: Gijs van Dam
Original format: Talpa Content B.V.
Licence: Talpa Distribution B.V.
Photographer: Roy Beusker

Client: It's My Party
Agency: GJP Advertising + Design
Creative directors: Lisa Greenberg,
Trevor Schoenfeld
Art director: Irene Pau
Copywriter: Kristofer Richardson

J
Client: JAKPETZ
Title: 'Crawling'
Agency: Saatchi & Saatchi Jakarta
Chief creative officer: Andy Greenaway
Executive creative director: Juhi Kalia
Art directors: Aryanto Salim, Joel Clement
Copywriters: Pancaputera, Juhi Kalia
Photographer: Heret Frasthio

Client: Jung von Matt/next GmbH
Title: 'Tagged in Motion'
Creative director: Simone Ashoff
Idea/concept/production: Nina Borrusch
Graffiti artist: Mirko Reisser
Programmer: Christoph Maeschig
Project managers: Dorte Luecker,
Thomas Kreutzer
Film production: Frank Zerban
Copywriter: Henning Korb

Title: Junk Food
Credits: Anton Alvarez, Yuko Maki,
Robert Ek, Olle Gustafsson, Jaya Karlsson

K
Client: K2 Ski
Concept and design: MBCO Team
Styling/decoration: Koenig Styling
Fair: ISPO 2/2007
Photographer: Peter Schaffrath

Client: Kawasaki City Museum
Title: 'Writing Lights, Lighting Write'
Design: Matzda Office Co., Ltd.
Designer: Yukimasa Matsuda

Client: K-Fee
Title: 'Explosion'
Agency: Jung von Matt/Fleet, Hamburg
Creative directors: Arno Lindemann,
Bernhard Lukas
Art director: Hendrik Schweder
Copywriter: Teja Fischer
Photographer: Jan Kornstaedt

Client: Kimberly-Clark Trading
Title: 'Oil', 'Wine', 'Coffee'
Product: Scott Kitchen Towels
Agency: JWT Kuala Lumpur
Executive creative director: Edwin Leong
Creative director: Hasnah Mohd Samidin
Art director: Yan Chay
Copywriters: Danie Kee, Jackson Mah,
Edwin Leong, Hasnah Mohd, Samidin
Photographer: Mak Kah Heng

Client: Kleenex
Title: 'Cup, Glass, Bowl, Spoon'
Product: Kleenex Kitchen Towels
Agency: JWT Beijing
Executive creative director: Jordan Hsueh
Creative director: Shankun Sun
Art director: Dechun Qiu
Copywriter: Su Wang

Client: KMCV
Title: 'Hands'
Agency: Magma Istanbul
Creative director: Irem Goren
Art directors: Cihangir Gumus, Arman Akıncı
Copywriters: Elif Sakallı, Izgi Tarakcioglu
Graphic designers: Cigdem Ozer, Murat Eser
Client relations: Alev Celiktas, Piraye Erdogan

Designer: Koiwai Reiko
Bag photographs: Foton Co., Ltd.
(Iwamoto Kenichi, Saburi Hisanori)
Animal photographs: Corbis Japan, Inc.
CG producer: Foton Co., Ltd.(Kaneko Kent)
CG: Foton Co., Ltd. (Hayashi Toshiyuki,
Onoda Keiko)

Title: Kvadrat Clouds
Credits: Kvadrat A/S
Design: Ronan and Erwan Bouroullec

Client: Kymyka
Title: Kymyka – Shoes and Bags
Design: Maurice Mentjens Design
Electric installations: Lejeune Multi Electra
Climate control: Lemmens Meesen
Lighting: Rexel Nederland
Floor: Smeets Stein Groep
Painting: Stones Onderhoud Service
Interior: Schreurs Interieur Timmerbedrijf,
Cadier en Keer
Magnets: M. Van der Schans B.V.,
Krimpen a/d Ijssel
Poles: Hellebeuk B.V., Hulsberg
Graphic design: Groenergras
Photographer: Arjen Schmitz

L
Client: LACOSTE
Title: Zaha Hadid for LACOSTE Footwear
Design: Zaha Hadid Architects

Client: Langland
Project: Langland Offices
Architects: Jump Studios (Shaun Fernandes,
Markus Nonn, Go Sugimoto)
Contractors: The Interiors Group
M&E: Callisia, KLEC
Office furniture systems and chairs by Steelcase

Client: Langmanyishen Limited Company
Title: Romanticism2 boutique
Design firm: SKSK architects
Designers: Keiichiro Sako, Takeshi Ishizaka
Photography: Koji Fujii/Nacása & Partners Inc.

Client: Legal Sea Foods
Title: Newspaper ad
Agency: DeVito/Verdi
Art directors/copywriters: Alexei Beltrone,
Jay Marsen
Creative director: Sal DeVito

Title: *LEGO-SHOW* (Sat.1)
Production: ProSieben Sat.1 Media AG
Host: Kai Pflaume

Client: LEGO Systems, Inc.
Title: Power Miners – 'Rock Rocket'
Agency: Blackdot

Client: Lenovo (Germany) GmbH
Agency: agencyteam Stuttgart GmbH
Senior copywriter: Corinna Peters
Senior account manager: Antonella Vasile
Creative director (art): Ian Spehr
Creative director (copy): Henning Mayer

Credits: LICHTFAKTOR
Title: Lightwriting
www.lichtfaktor.eu

Client: Lion Nathan
Title: Speight's Great Beer Delivery
Product: Speight's Beer
Agency: Publicis Mojo, Auckland
Executive creative director: Corey Esse
Executive creative director/copywriter:
Nick Worthington
Art directors: Lachlan McPherson,
Lorenz Perry
Copywriters: Karl Fleet, Guy Denniston
Photographer: Ross Brown

Title: *LittleBigPlanet*
Publisher: Sony Computer Entertainment
Developer: Media Molecule

Title: London College of Fashion –
Graduate Exhibition
Client: London College of Fashion
Creative director: David Eveleigh-Evans
Designer: Davin Gormley
Creative programmer: Karsten Schmidt
Producer: Paul Albert
Design group: Moving Brands
Project manager: Paul Martin
Marketing manager: Anna Millhouse

Title: LUMINEX® patented fabric and products
Credits: LUMINEX S.p.A.

Client: Lürzer's Archive Student Contest 2007
Title: 'Heidi and Clara'
Credits: Mark Haefele
(AAA School of Advertising)

Client: Lush Lawn and Property Enhancement
Title: Lush Business Card
Agency: Struck
Executive creative director: Steve Driggs
Copywriter: Rich Black
Art director: Brandon Knowlden
Printer: Athenaeum Press

M
Client: Madrid City Council
Title: 'The Wishing Tree'
Agency: Marketingvivo Madrid
Executive creative director:
Sergio Rosenblat
Art director: Luciana Comes
Media manager: Paloma Granero
Strategic planner: Juan Daniel Sever

Title: Map of the Internet
Photo credit: Matt Britt and Barrett Lyon

Client: McDonald's
Title: 'Extra Large Coffee'
Agency: DDB Stockholm
Creative director: Andreas Dahlqvist
Art directors: Simon Higby, Ted Harry
Mellström, Viktor Arve
Copywriter: Martin Lundgren

Client: McDonald's/Coca-Cola
Title: 'Coca-Cola – Stairs vs. Escalator'
Product: Coca-Cola Light
Agency: DDB Stockholm
Creative director: Andreas Dahlqvist
Art directors/copywriters: Simon Higby,
Viktor Arve, Felix Soderlind, Tove Eriksen
Photographer: Alexander Pihl

Client: Mercedes-Benz
Title: BAS Plus, Read the Street: 'Child',
'Ball' and 'Dog'
Agency: BBDO Düsseldorf GmbH
Creative directors: Toygar Bazarkaya,
Ton Hollander
Art director: Sven Klasen
Copywriters: Markus Steinkemper,
Toni Selzer

Client: Microsoft
Title: *Gears of War*
Credits: Kumar Manix, Rinsed Studio

Client: Microsoft
Credits: Joanne Liddell, Richard Hirst
(Microsoft), Michael Chugg (Chugg
Entertainment), Mark Pope (Mark Pope
Music), Tanya Pedashanko (Pulse
Communications), Nic Lloyd (Triangle
Communications), Lisa Ince (Sydney
Promotional Dancers), Simon Micarone
(Rinsed Studio)

Title: Milk Desk
Designer: Søren Rose
www.sorenrose.com
Photographers: Søren Rønholt
(Aquarium, Trashcan)/Jens Stoltze
(Box, Full Macsetup, Slot)

Client: MindLab
Title: MindLab Office
Photographer: Anne Mie Dreves
Original design: Bosch & Fjord
Redesign: (Identity) Allthewaytoparis.com
http://allthewaytoparis.com/2008/04/21/
mindlab-identity/ and Nord Arkitekter
(nord-web.dk)

Client: MINI
Title: Mini – AutoRai Tradeshow
Company: Cees Smit
Creatives: Hypsos

Client: MINI
Product: Mini Cabrio
Title: www.mini.de/webcam –
Augmented Reality Campaign
Idea, concept and realization:
Buzzin Monkey
PR and marketing: die agentour
Online special: Interone, Hamburg

Credits: MisoSoupDesign
Title: POrOus chair
Designed by: Daisuke Nagatomo

Client: Mondo Pasta
Title: 'Noodle Slurper'
Agency: Jung von Matt
Creative directors: Jan Rexhausen,
Doerte Spengler-Ahrens

Client: Moroso
Title: 'Caged Beauty', Interieur Kortrijk 2006,
Belgium
Design: Studio Arne Quinze
www.studioarnequinze.tv

Client: MTV
Title: MTV Video Music Awards 2006 New York
Design: Stufish – The Mark Fisher Studio

Client: Muji
Title: Muji – Light bulb packaging/lampshade
Design agency: SiebertHead Ltd,
London, UK
Designer: Ben Cox

N

Title: National Gallery Grand Tour
Client: Danielle Chidlow (The National
Gallery), Dan Gates (Hewlett Packard)
Agency: The Partners
Strategic consultant: Jim Prior
Art director: Greg Quinton
Project managers: Donna Hemley,
Andrew Webster
Design director: Robert Ball
Designers: Kevin Lan, Paul Currah
Copywriter: Jim Davis

Client: Natural Crisps Limited
Title: Jonathan Crisp
Agency: Ziggurat Brand Consultants
Creative director: Allison Miguel
Designer: Hayley Bishop

Client: NBC Universal Global Networks
Deutschland GmbH
Title: 'Blood Bath'
Product/Service: 13TH STREET
Advertising agency/web design agency:
Jung von Matt AG
Creative director: Bernd Kraemer
Designer: Felix Schulz
Project managers: Sebastian Schimpeler,
Helen Seiffe
Copywriter: Henning Korb
Illustrator: Moritz Schmidt
Technical realization: Maximilian Lips,
Jan Singelmann

Title: Neuronal Circuit
Credits: Paul De Koninck,
www.greenspine.ca

Client: Nestlé Peters
Title: Summer Madness Memorial Statues
Product: Frosty Fruits
Agency: Publicis Mojo, Melbourne
Creative director: Leon Wilson
Creatives: Lea Egan, Jonty Bell
Character design: Wilfrid Wood

Client: New Zealand Transport Agency
Title: 'Intersections, Crumpled Car'
Agency: Clemenger BBDO
Creative director: Philip Andrew
Creative director/art director: Mark Haricks
Art director/copywriter: Brigid Alkema

Client: Nissan
Title: 'Qashqai: Urban Proof'
Product: Qashqai
Agency: TBWA\Paris
Creative director, Nissan: Chris Garbutt
Art director: Philippe Taroux
Copywriter: Benoit Leroux
Photographer: Greg White
3D & post-production: Taylor James

Title: Nissan NV200
Design: Nissan Design Center/Nissan Design
Europe (London)
Creative director: Shiro Nakamura

Client: Novartis
Product: Otrivin
Agency: Saatchi & Saatchi, Milan
Executive creative directors:
John Pallant, Roger Kennedy, Olivier Girard,
Jean-François Fournon
Creative directors: Guido Cornara,
Agostino Toscana
Art director: Luca Pannese
Copywriter: Luca Lorenzini
Illustrator: Rob Perry
Photographer: Davide Bodini

Client: Nutella – Ferrero Spa.
Title: 1st prizewinner, Design for Nutella
contest, run by *Interni* magazine & Ferrero
Design: Alessandro Stabile and Isaac Piñeiro
School: Scuola Politécnica di Design, Milan
Professor: Odoardo Fioravanti

O

Title: Office in a Bucket (OIAB)
Designed and manufactured by:
Inflate, London

Title: Open-Heart Surgery
Credits:
www.flickr.com/photos/yelverton/113473863/

Client: Oral-B
Title: 'Meat'/'Seafood'/'Vegetable'
Agency: Ogilvy & Mather, Seoul
Chief creative officer: Wain Choi
Creative director: Yongsun Kim
Art director: Jongok Shin
Copywriter: Sunbok Lee
Graphic designer: Jinwoo Kwon

Client: Osiris
Title: 'Bronx' Shoebox
Designer: Nick Simon
Additional credits: Dyse One, Kyle Klem
www.nicksimon.net

Company: Outline Innovation B.V.
Title: Wine In A Can
Designers: Jens Andersson, Jonas Forsman
www.outlineinnovation.com

P
Client: Palotta TeamWorks
Title: Container Office
Design: Clive Wilkinson Architects

Client: Pet & Breakfast
Title: 'Cheetah'
Agency: Lowe Amsterdam
Art director: Maarten Vrouwes
Copywriter: Friso Ludenhoff
Retoucher: Magic
Agency producer: Mirijam van der Werff

Project: Pitti Uomo Fashion Fair Fall/Winter
2009–2010
Client: Thom Browne
Credits: Villa Eugénie
Location: Fortessa di Basso, Florence, Italy
(Istituto di Scienze Militari Aeronautiche)
Photography: By2Photographers

Title: PODLE™
Credits: Nouvel Œuvre

Client: Pon's Automobielhandel
Title: 'Product Recall'
Agency: DDB Amsterdam
Creative directors: Dylan de Backer, Joris Kuijpers
Art director: Joris Kuijpers
Copywriter: Dylan de Backer

Client: Prada
Design: OMA
Project: Asian Pavilion for Prada
Status: Concept Design 2008
Location: Seoul, South Korea
Partners: Rem Koolhaas, Ellen van Loon
Associates: Kunle Adeyemi, Kees van Casteren,
Chris van Duijn
Design architect: Alexander Reichert
with Hyoeun Kim, Ye Rin Kang, Vincent
McIlduff, David Moon, Mariano Sagasta,
Claudia Romao, Eva Dietrich, Alex de Jong,
Wayne Congar, Miguel Huelga de la Fuente,
Gustavo Paternina-Soberon, Nam Joo Kim

Client: Print it!
Title: 'Hand to Hand'
Creatives: María de Ros Padrós (architect),
Daniel Loewe (photography)
Art and design director: María de Ros Padrós
Photography director: Daniel Loewe
Location: Casa Decor Madrid
Photographer: Daniel Loewe

Client: Procter & Gamble
Title: 'Ariel 20°' direct mail
Product: Ariel
Agency: Saatchi & Saatchi, Frankfurt
Chief creative officer: Burkhart von Scheven
Creative directors: Florian Pagel,
Eberhard Kirchhoff, Folker Wrage
Art director: Anna-Marina Pirsch
Copywriter: Philipp Böttcher

Client: Procter & Gamble
Title: Charmin NYC Restroom Experience
Agency: Gigunda Group, Inc.

Client: Procter & Gamble
Title: 'Tide – Loads of Hope'
Agency: Saatchi & Saatchi, New York
EVP, NA creative director: Audrey Huffenreuter
Planning director: Wanda Pogue
Audio engineer: Rick Oakley

Client: Procter & Gamble
Product: Tide
Title: 'The Luminous Whites'
Agency: Leo Burnett, Moscow
Creative director: Mikhail Kudashkin
Art director: Alexandra Scherbovich
Copywriters: Polina Bogatyreva-Maguire,
Viktor Lander

Client: PROJEKTPILOT GmbH
Title: PROJEKTPILOT GmbH | EuroShop 2008
Design: D'art Design Gruppe
Photographer: Joerg Hempel Photodesign

Client: Puma
Title: 'Pumus Trendycus'
Agency: Bruketa & Îiniç OM
Creative director: Moe Minkara
Art director, designer: Petar Popoviç
Copywriter: Kitica Kekiç, Studio Kapulica
Account executive: Marija Jakeljiç

R
Title: R21
Credits: Cohda Studio/Richard Liddle

Client: RAPP Colombia
Title: Rapp Collins flat mailing:
'Our Customers Stick To Us'
Agency: RAPP Colombia
Creative director: Pablo Castro
General creative director: Juan David Botero
Art director: Yesid Suárez
Graphic designer: Javier Clavijo
Copywriter: Martha Hernández
Account executives: Ana Milena Díaz,
Ana María Lozano

Title: Recycled Tube Light
Credits: Castor
Designers: Brian Richer, Kei Ng
Photographer: Ryan Taylor/Castor Design

Credits: Red Bull
Event: Red Bull Air Race World Championships
2009 – Windsor
Athlete: Paul Bonhomme
Photo credit: © Garth Milan/
Red Bull Photofiles
Location: Windsor, Ontario, Canada

Credits: Red Bull
Event: Red Bull Air Race WS 2008 – Rotterdam
Athlete: Mike Goulian
Photo credit: © Predrag Vuckovic/
Red Bull Photofiles
Location: Rotterdam, Netherlands

Credits: Red Bull
Event: Channel Crossing 2003
Athlete: Felix Baumgartner
Discipline: Parachuting
Photo credit: © ulrichgrill.com/
Red Bull Photofiles
Location: Calais, France

Credits: Red Bull
Event: Red Bull Crashed Ice
Athlete: Event Participants
Discipline: Ice Cross Downhill
Photo credit: © Jörg Mitter/Red Bull Photofiles
Location: Place de la Riponne, Lausanne,
Switzerland

Title: Re-Inventing Functionality
Credits: Joris Laarman
Photographer: Rik Seisveld
Courtesy of Droog Collection

Client: Rémy Cointreau
Title: 'Piper Heidsieck – Rosé Sauvage'
by Viktor & Rolf
Design: Sleever International

Client: Renault Clio Sport
Agency: Nordpol + Hamburg
Title: 'Renault Clio – The Game'
www.clio.de/thegame/en

Client: Replay
Title: 25th Anniversary
Agency: JOSEPH ROSSI srl
Creative director/art director: Joseph Rossi
Design: Graphic First Aid

Client: The Rolling Stones
Title: The Rolling Stones: *A Bigger Bang*
Tour 2005
Design: Stufish – The Mark Fisher Studio

Client: RTL/PLUG TV
Title: PLUG TV
Agency: SEVEN
Creative director: Sven Mastbooms
Production: Seven
Director: Zanadu, Tom Willems
DOP: Anton Mertens
Art direction and character design:
Dimitri De Cooman, Sven Mastbooms,
Bart Ribbens
Editing and post-production: Bert Jacobs,
Bart Ribbens
Animation: Bart Ribbens, Dimitri De Cooman

S
Client: Samsung
Title: 'Extreme LED Sheep Art'
Agency: The Viral Factory

Client: Samsung Tesco
Title: HomePlus Supermarket
Agency: CHEIL WORLDWIDE, Seoul
Executive creative director: Ina Choi
Creative director: Yooshin Lee
Art directors: Kangwook Lee, Chaehoon Lee,
Yooho Lee, Sanghun Yoo
Copywriter: Jungho Hwang, Sua Lee
Illustrator: Bom Communication

Client: Sharp Electronics
Title: 'Bloom'
Design: Tronic Studio
Curator: Formavision
Ad agency: Wieden+Kennedy
Manufacturer: Kreysler & Associates

Title: skinnyCorp/Threadless Office
Credits: skinnyCorp/Threadless

Credits: Emma Smart
Title: Lunchboxes

Title: Solar Bottle
Designed by: Alberto Meda & Francisco
Gomez Paz

Client: Sony Computer Entertainment
Title: 'Handcuffs'
Agency: TBWA\ESPAÑA, Madrid
Creative directors: Juan Sánchez, Guillermo
Ginés, Montse Pastor, Vicente Rodríguez,
Bernardo Hernández
Art director: Bernardo Hernández

Product: Sour Marbels
Client: Perfetti van Melle, India
Agency: Ogilvy & Mather, Mumbai
Executive chairman/National creative
director: Piyush Pandey
Executive creative directors: Abhijit Avasthi,
Rajiv Rao
Creative director: Anurag Agnihotri
Art director: Ashish Naik
Copywriters: Saurabh Kulkarni,
Nasrullah Husami
Illustrator: Deelip Khomane
Typographer: Ashish Naik
Account supervisor: Lavanya Anirudh
Account managers: Antara Suri, Manan Shah

Client: Spar European Shopping
Centers GmbH
Idea: Marcus Wild
Concept: Christoph Andexlinger
Architecture: Massimiliano Fuksas
Programme director: Margret Stronegger
Marketing: Brigitte Biberger

Client: SPCA
Title: 'A Very Silent Night'
Agency: DraftFCB New Zealand
Executive creative director: James Mok
Creatives: Alex Dyer, Colin Mitchell
Production company: The Film Brewery
Director: Chris Graham
Production company producer:
Treza Gallogly
Composition: Digital Post
Sound engineer: Bruno Barrett-Garnier

Client: Spoetzl Brewery/Shiner Beer
Title: Shiner Beer Koozies & Outdoor
Campaign
Agency: McGarrah Jessee, Austin, Texas
Creative directors: Cameron Day,
James Mikus
Art directors: Beau Hanson, Michael Anderson
Copywriter: Tannen Campbell

Client: Spontex
Title: 'Hand Care'
Agency: Reskala y Asociados, Mexico
Creative director: Joan Cordoves
Art directors: Enrique Guzmán, Adriana Romero
Copywriters: Joan Cordoves,
Enrique Guzmán, Eduardo Prieto
Account executives: Adriana Deza,
Araceli Avalos

Title: STICK tea
Credits: STICK tea

Title: Strandbeest
Design by: Theo Jansen

Client: Studio Brussel
Title: 'Black Boy Wanting Water'
Agency: MortierBrigade
Creative directors: Jens Mortier, Joost Berends,
Philippe Deceuster
Copywriters/art directors: Tim Driesen,
Joeri Vandenbroeck, Dieter Vanhoof

Credits: Studio Tord Boontje
Petit Jardin Bench, 2006 – Design by Studio
Tord Boontje, limited edition of 10.
Petit Jardin Armchair, 2006 – Design by Studio
Tord Boontje, limited edition of 10.

Client: Suzusen
Title: Crocodile Leather Bag, 'Zebra'
Agency: Grey Tokyo
Creative director: Soeda Masayoshi
Art director: Iwamoto Takeshi
Copywriter: Oki Kei

Client: Swarovski
Title: Swarovski Crystal Palace 'Stardust'
Design: Tokujin Yoshioka Design
Photos: Nacasa & Partners Inc.

Client: Syngenta Crop Protection
Title: Syngenta PortA Pac
Company: pi global
Technical director: Jed O'Brien
Production director: Eric Connolly
Development engineer: Dave Salmon

T

Client: TAISUN Enterprise Co., Ltd.
Title: 'Water Infinity'
Design company: creative XAN
Corporation
Creative director: Alex Su
Designer: Tatsuya Kobayashi
3D computer graphics: Jessy Lee

Client: Target
Title: 'Art Connects'
Agency: Catalyst Studios
Client creative director: Ron Anderson
Agency creative director: Shannon Pettini
Campaign strategy director: Betsy Treinen

Client: tesa AG
Title: 'Tape Art®'
Product: tesapack® ultra strong
Agency: Jung von Matt/Neckar GmbH
Creative directors: Joachim Silber,
Michael Ohanian, Mark Khaisman
Art director: Stefan Roesinger
Copywriters: Lennart Frank,
Tassilo Gutscher
Illustrator: Mark Khaisman
Graphic designer: Dominic Stuebler
Account executive: Harald Isenmann

Client: Tesco
Title: Tesco Tortilla Range
Design agency: P&W Design
Photographer: Laurie Evans
Art directors: Pemberton & Whitefoord
Designer: Barry Crombie
Design director: Simon Pemberton

Client: *The Times of India*
Title: 'DO!'
Agency: JWT, Mumbai, India
Creative directors: Agnello Dias,
Debu Purkayastha, Vistasp Hodiwala,
Arkadyuti Basu, Vinayak Gaikwad

Client: Toyota
Title: Toyota iQ OOH
Agency: Dentsu, Tokyo
Creative director: Naoya Hosokawa
Art director: Takahiro Tsuchiya

Client: Toyota
Title: 2010 Toyota Prius Microsite
www.toyota.com/vehicles/minisite/
newprius/#/pre-collision-system/
Agency: EVB and Saatchi & Saatchi,
Los Angeles
Executive creative director (EVB):
Stephen Goldblatt
Interactive creative director (Saatchi):
Scott Huebscher
Senior designer (EVB): Steven Knodel
Art director (Saatchi): Nick Luckett
Copywriter (Saatchi): Eric Burnett
Designer (EVB): Enrique Camacho
Technical lead (EVB)/Flash programmer (EVB):
Brad Griffin
Director of technology (EVB): Husani Oakley

Client: Toyota
Title: Toyota iQ OOH
Agency: Dentsu, Tokyo
Creative director: Naoya Hosokawa
Art director: Takahiro Tsuchiya

Title: T_Pod
Art director: Elisabeth Soós.
Designers: Elisabeth Soós, Florian Nissl

Client: Tracfone
Brand: NET10
Title: 'Microwave'
Agency: Droga5
Executive creative directors: Ted Royer,
Duncan Marshall
Copywriter: Kevin Brady
Art director: Alex Lea
Production company: Smuggler
Post-production: The Mill
Lead flame artist: Phil Crowe
Flame artists: Corey Brown, Paul Kirsch,
Dan Williams
Puppet design: Stan Winston

Client: TV6
Title: 'The Weed-o-Gram'
Agency: Le Bureau
Creatives: Jonas Wittenmark,
Tobias Carlson, Claes Kjellström
Agency producer: Nina Malén
Account handler: Gustaf Sehlstedt

Client: TVNZ
Title: 'Around the World in 80 Days'
Agency: Saatchi & Saatchi NZ, Auckland
Executive creative director:
Mike O'Sullivan
Creatives: Tim Howman, Bex Radford
General manager: Sonya Berrigan
Group account director: Jillian Stanton
Account director: Sarah Maclean
Design: The Craftshop
Head of marketing and emerging business
(TVNZ): Jason Paris
TV2 marketing manager (TVNZ):
Jodi O'Donnell

Client: Tzabar Travel Agency
Brand: Tzabar Show
Campaign: 'Who Knows – Britney/Amy'
Agency: Grey, Tel Aviv
Executive creative director: Yonatan Stirin
Creative directors: Shani Gershi,
Ronen Gur-Fonarov
Art directors/copywriters: Asaf Levi, Eran Nir
Illustrators: Eitay Reichert (Britney),
Gili Comforty (Amy)

U

Client: Unilever
Title: 'The Fixer Show'
Product: Axe
Production company: Mekanism, San Francisco
Director: Tommy Means
Executive producer: Jason Harris
Creative director/copywriter:
Andre Ricciardi
Producer: Elizabeth Morse
Art: Scott Barry
DP: Andy Lilien
Editor: Ed Feldman
Site programming: Rokkan, David Cole
Production design: David Dougherty
Motion graphics: Courtney Booker
Director of development: Jamal Berkeley
Mixing: Studio Guapo, Chris Forrest

Client: Unilever
Title: 'Axe Hair Crisis Relief, 100 Girls'
Product: Axe
Agency: BBH New York
Production company: B-Reel
Creative directors: Calle Sjoenell,
Pelle Sjoenell
Chief creative: Kevin Roddy
Art director: Erik Holmdahl
Copywriter: Beth Ryan

Client: Unilever Thailand
Title: 'Torture Test'
Product: Breeze Excel
Agency: Lowe Bangkok
Creative directors: Clinton Manson,
Dominic Stallard
Art director: Dominic Stallard
Copywriter: Clinton Manson
Production house: Remix Studio Bangkok

Client: Urban Decay
Title: 'Pocket Rocket'
Design: HCT Packaging/Urban Decay

Title: U.R.E. Live
Credits: Cohda Studio/Richard Liddle

V
Client: Venti Eventi
Title: 'Dispatchwork'
Design by: Jan Vormann

Credits: Village Underground
Photographer: Light and Time © 2006-9

Title: Volivik chandelier
Credits: Estudio enPieza

Client: Volkswagen
Title: 'Overtake Faster'
Agency: DDB Düsseldorf
Creative directors: Heiko Freyland, Raphael
Milczarek, Alexander Reiss
Art directors: Raphael Milczarek,
Fabian Kirner, Michael Kittel
Copywriters: Heiko Freyland, Felix Lemcke,
Jan Propach, Shahir Sirry

W
Client: Watsons Water
Title: 'Water'
Design: Kan & Lau Design Consultants

Client: WB&CO Organic Vegetable Juice
www.wildbunchandcompany.com
Studio: SEED Creative Consultants
London & Singapore
Designers: Mark Walker & Garnet Teo;
www.seed.uk.com
Photographer: www.milkphotographie.com

Client: Weingut M. Machalek
Agency/design: Max Jurasch
Title: Wine Labels/Calendar Sheet
www.jurasch.com

Title: WiiSpray 2nd edition
Design: Martin Lihs
Photographer: Jens Hauspurg

Title: Worldwide Pillow Fight Club 2009
Location: Vancouver, Canada
Photographer: Kevin Wu

Client: World Wildlife Fund Beijing
Title: 'Target Practice'
Agency: Ogilvy & Mather, Beijing
Creative director: Jacky Lung
Art directors: Jacky Lung, Shengxiong Chen
Photographer: Huimin Li

X
Credits: Xosé Teiga
Title: Self-promotion

Y
Client: Y3
Credits: Villa Eugénie
Project: Y3 – Fall Winter 07/08 Fashion Show
Event: Fashion Show
Location: Hunter College, New York
Photography: By2Photographers

Nicolai Andler
*Tools for Project Management, Workshops
and Consulting: A Must-Have Compendium
of Essential Tools and Techniques*
Erlangen: Publicis, 2008

Christopher M. Avery
*Teamwork Is an Individual Skill: Getting Your
Work Done When Sharing Responsibility*
San Francisco: Berrett-Koehler, 2001

Klaus Backhaus, Joachim Büschken,
Markus Voeth
International Marketing
Basingstoke: Houndmills; New York:
Palgrave Macmillan, 2005

Pete Barry
*The Advertising Concept Book:
Think Now, Design Later*
London: Thames & Hudson, 2008

Trevor J. Bentley
Sharpen Your Team's Skills in Creativity
London: McGraw-Hill, 1997

Scott Berkun
The Myths of Innovation
Sebastopol, CA: O'Reilly Media, 2007

George M. Beylerian, Andrew Dent
*Ultra Materials: How Materials Innovation
is Changing the World*
London: Thames & Hudson, 2007

Chris Bilton
*Management and Creativity: From Creative
Industries to Creative Management*
Oxford: Blackwell, 2007

Christian Bjone
*Art and Architecture: Strategies
in Collaboration*
Basel and Boston: Birkhäuser, 2009

Simon Bley
*Open Innovation in der Automobilindustrie –
Möglichkeiten und Grenzen*
Saarbrücken: VDM Verlag Dr. Müller, 2009

Gernot Brauer
*Dynaform + Cube: Architecture as Brand
Communication*
Basel and Boston: Birkhäuser, 2002

Tim Brown
*Change by Design: How Design Thinking
Transforms Organizations and Inspires
Innovation*
New York: HarperCollins, 2009

Bernhard E. Bürdek
*Design: History, Theory, and Practice
of Product Design*
Boston: Birkhäuser, 2005

Richard E. Caves
*Creative Industries: Contracts Between
Art and Commerce*
Cambridge, MA and London:
Harvard University Press, 2000

Alexander Chernev
Strategic Marketing Management
Chicago: Brightstar Media, 2006

Henry Chesbrough, Wim Vanhaverbeke,
Joel West
Open Innovation: Researching a New Paradigm
Oxford: Oxford University Press, 2006

Clayton M. Christensen, Michael Overdorf,
Stefan Thomke (eds.)
Harvard Business Review on Innovation
Cambridge, MA: Harvard Business School
Press, 2001

John L. Colley Jr, Jacqueline L. Doyle,
George W. Logan, Wallace Stettinius
Corporate Governance
New York: McGraw-Hill, 2003

Thomas H. Davenport, Laurence Prusak
*Working Knowledge: How Organizations
Manage What They Know*
Boston, MA: Harvard Business Press, 1998

Tony Davila, Robert Shelton,
Marc J. Epstein
*Making Innovation Work: How to
Manage It, Measure It, and Profit from It*
Upper Saddle River, NJ: Wharton
School Pub., 2006

Martin J. Eppler
*Managing Information Quality: Increasing the
Value of Information in Knowledge-Intensive
Products and Processes*
Berlin and London: Springer, 2003

Jean-Louis Ferrier
Picasso, la déconstruction créatrice
Paris: Terrail, 1993

Heinz von Foerster, Ernst von Glasersfeld,
Peter M. Hejl
Einführung in den Konstruktivismus
Munich: R. Oldenbourg, 1985

Jack Foster, Larry Corby
How to Get Ideas
San Francisco, CA: Berrett-Koehler, 2007

Peter A. Gloor
*Swarm Creativity: Competitive Advantage
Through Collaborative Innovation Networks*
Oxford and New York: Oxford University
Press, 2006

Lynda Gratton
*Living Strategy: Putting People at
the Heart of Corporate Purpose*
Harlow: Pearson Education Ltd, 2000

John H. Hartley
Creative Industries
Malden, MA and Oxford: Blackwell, 2005

Gerhard Heufler
Design Basics: From Ideas to Products
Sulgen: Niggli Verlag, 2004

James M. Higgins
Strategic Management: Text and Cases
Chicago and London: Dryden, 1989

Tom Himpe
Advertising is Dead, Long Live Advertising!
London: Thames & Hudson, 2008

Tom Himpe
*Advertising Next: 150 Winning Campaigns
for the New Communications Age*
London: Thames & Hudson, 2008

John Howkins
*The Creative Economy:
How People Make Money From Ideas*
London: Allen Lane, 2001

John Kao
*Innovation Nation: How America Is Losing
Its Innovation Edge, Why It Matters,
and What We Can Do To Get It Back*
New York and London: Free Press, 2007

Werner Kroeber-Riel, Franz-Rudolf Esch,
Richard Köhler, Heribert Meffert,
Hermann Diller
*Strategie und Technik der Werbung:
Verhaltenswissenschaftliche Ansätze*
Stuttgart: Kohlhammer, 1991

Blandine Laperche, Dimitri Uzunidis,
Nick von Tunzelmann (eds.)
*The Genesis of Innovation: Systemic Linkages
Between Knowledge and the Market*
Cheltenham: Edward Elgar, 2008

Steven D. Levitt, Stephen J. Dubner
*Freakonomics: A Rogue Economist
Explores the Hidden Side of Everything*
London: Allen Lane, 2005

Gavin Lucas, Mike Dorrian
*Guerrilla Advertising: Unconventional
Brand Communication*
London: Laurence King, 2006

Steven P. MacGregor, Teresa Torres-Coronas
*Higher Creativity for Virtual Teams:
Developing Platforms for Co-Creation*
Hershey, PA: Information Science
Reference, 2007

Alan McKinlay, Chris Smith (eds.)
*Creative Labour: Working in
the Creative Industries*
Basingstoke: Palgrave Macmillan, 2009

Fredmund Malik
*Effective Top Management: Beyond
the Failure of Corporate Governance
and Shareholder Value*
Weinheim: Wiley-VCH, 2006

Fredmund Malik
*Strategie des Managements komplexer
Systeme: Ein Beitrag zur Management-
Kybernetik evolutionärer Systeme*
Berne: P. Haupt, 1984

Daniela Manger
*Innovation und Kooperation: Zur
Organisierung eines regionalen Netzwerks*
Bielefeld: Transcript, 2009

Jeff Mauzy, Richard Harriman
*Creativity, Inc.: Building an Inventive
Organization*
Boston: Harvard Business School, 2003

Georges Merx
*Soft Skills for Software Engineers:
The People Side of Technology Management*
San Diego: 963 Publishing Company, 2007

Stephen Nachmanovitch
Free Play: Improvisation in Life and Art
Los Angeles: J.P. Tarcher, 1990

Helga Nowotny
*Insatiable Curiosity: Innovation
in a Fragile Future*
Cambridge, MA and London: MIT, 2008

Wally Olins
The Brand Handbook
London: Thames & Hudson, 2008

Brian Po-Yen Lee, Chien-Hsu Chen
*The Impact of Case-Based Visual Stimuli
on Conceptual Design Creativity*
Saarbrücken: VDM Verlag Dr. Müller, 2008

C. K. Prahalad
*The New Age of Innovation: Driving
Co-Created Value Through Global Networks*
New York and London: McGraw-Hill, 2008

Mario Pricken
*Creative Advertising: Ideas and Techniques
from the World's Best Campaigns*
London: Thames & Hudson, 2008

Mario Pricken, Christine Klell
*Visual Creativity: Inspirational Ideas for
Advertising, Animation and Digital Design*
London: Thames & Hudson, 2004

Gilbert Probst, Steffen Raub, Kai Romhardt
*Managing Knowledge: Building
Blocks for Success*
New York: Wiley, 1999

Garr Reynolds
*Presentation Zen: Simple Ideas on
Presentation Design and Delivery*
Berkeley, CA: New Riders, 2008

Everett M. Rogers
Diffusion of Innovations
New York: Free Press of Glencoe;
London: Macmillan, 1962

Michael L. Stallard
*Fired Up or Burned Out: How to
Reignite Your Team's Passion,
Creativity and Productivity*
Nashville, TN: Thomas Nelson, 2007

Bettina von Stamm
Managing Innovation, Design and Creativity
Chichester: Wiley, 2003

Mark Stefik, Barbara Stefik
*Breakthrough: Stories and Strategies
of Radical Innovation*
Cambridge, MA: MIT Press, 2004

Uwe Stoklossa
*Advertising: New Techniques
for Visual Seduction*
London: Thames & Hudson, 2007

Don Tapscott, Anthony D. Williams
*Wikinomics: How Mass Collaboration
Changes Everything*
New York: Portfolio; London: Penguin, 2006

Leigh L. Thompson, Hoon-Seok Choi (eds.)
*Creativity and Innovation in
Organizational Teams*
Mahwah, NJ: Lawrence Erlbaum
Associates, 2006

Joe Tidd, John Bessant
*Managing Innovation: Integrating
Technological, Market and
Organizational Change*
Chichester: Wiley, 1997

Peter Tschmuck
*Creativity and Innovation in
the Music Industry*
Dordrecht: Springer, 2006

Simon Veksner
How to Make It as an Advertising Creative
London: Laurence King, 2010

Frederic Vester
*Neuland des Denkens: vom technokratischen
zum kybernetischen Zeitalter*
Stuttgart: Deutsche Verlags-Anstalt, 1980

Paul Watzlawick
*How Real is Real?: Confusion,
Disinformation, Communication*
New York: Random House, 1976

Paul Watzlawick
*The Invented Reality: How Do We
Know What We Believe We Know?
Contributions to Constructivism*
New York and London: Norton, 1984

Michael West
*The Secrets of Successful Team Management:
How to Lead a Team to Innovation,
Creativity and Success*
London: Duncan Baird Publishers, 2004

Michael A. West
*Effective Teamwork: Practical Lessons
from Organizational Research*
Malden, MA and Oxford: BPS Blackwell, 2004

Helmut Willke
*Smart Governance: Governing the
Global Knowledge Society*
Frankfurt am Main: Campus, 2007

Marilyn Zelinsky
*The Inspired Workspace: Designs for
Creativity & Productivity*
Gloucester, MA: Rockport, 2004